HOMEMADE HEALTHY
DOG FOOD & TREATS COOKBOOK:

150+ Healthy, Fast, and Easy Recipes That Will Make Him Waggle His Tail! How to Cook 100% Natural and Vet-Approved Meals to Feed Your Furry Friend Safely

Martha B. Holland

Table of Contents

INTRODUCTION 5

CHAPTER 1: WHAT IS A HOMEMADE DOG FOOD DIET? 7

CHAPTER 2: THE BENEFITS OF HOMEMADE DOG FOOD DIET 8

- HEALTH REASONS 8
- VARIETY 8
- ELIMINATE ALLERGENS 8
- KNOWING WHAT THEY'RE TRULY EATING 9
- REGULATING FOOD QUALITY 9
- ELIMINATING FILLER INGREDIENTS 9
- FRESH, NOT PRESERVED FOOD 9
- A POTENTIALLY CHEAPER OPTION 9
- LESS WASTE 9
- NUTRITIONAL VALUE 10

CHAPTER 3: GUIDELINES TO FEED YOUR DOG 11

- HOW MUCH SHOULD MY DOG EAT? 11
- HOW OFTEN SHOULD YOU GIVE YOUR DOG FOOD? 12

CHAPTER 4: NUTRITIONAL GUIDELINES 13

- ESSENTIAL NUTRIENTS 14

CHAPTER 5: PROHIBITED FOODS 17

- RAISINS AND GRAPES 17
- CHERRIES 17
- NIGHTSHADE 17
- AVOCADO 17
- MUSHROOMS 17
- RHUBARB LEAF 18
- MACADAMIA 18
- XYLITOL 18
- NUTMEG 18
- CHOCOLATE 18
- GARLIC AND ONIONS 18
- ALCOHOL 18
- YEAST DOUGH 18

CHAPTER 6: MAKING YOUR OWN DOG FOOD 19

BREAKFAST DISHES 20

- 1. BERRY OATMEAL & PUMPKIN 21
- 2. SWEET POTATO & PEANUT BUTTER 21
- 3. PEANUT BUTTER MIX 21
- 4. DEVILED EGGS 22
- 5. MINI LIVER QUICHE 22
- 6. CHIA SEED OATMEAL 23
- 7. SPINACH OMELET 23
- 8. HOMEMADE DOG FRENCH OMELET 23
- 9. COTTAGE CHEESE BREAKFAST 24
- 10. BLUEBERRY MUFFIN 24
- 11. CARROT CAKE MUFFINS 25
- 12. MEAT DOG CAKE 25
- 13. MINI PUMPKIN MUFFINS 26
- 14. SCRAMBLED EGGS 26
- 15. APPLE DOG CAKES 27
- 16. HOMEMADE TURKEY OMELET 27
- 17. FISHERMEN'S EGGS 27
- 18. ALMOND AND BANANA TREATS 28

MAIN DISHES 29

- 19. BEEF AND SWEET POTATO STEW 30
- 20. CHICKEN SOUP 30
- 21. BROCCOLI BEEF WITH BARLEY 31
- 22. VEGETABLE BOWL 31
- 23. MAX AND PENNY'S SPINACH 32
- 24. PUMPKIN RICE 32

25. Tahini Fish … 33	60. Favorite gourmet meal … 47
26. Beef Stock … 33	61. Thanksgiving meal recipe … 48
27. Chicken Stew Meal … 34	62. Vegetable & Turkey Delight … 48
28. Turkey Jerky … 34	63. Gravy with Giblets … 49
29. Tofu and Tapioca … 35	64. Beef Stew … 49
30. Triple Three (Chicken, beef, salmon) … 35	65. Lamb Hash … 50
31. Pumpkin Balls … 35	66. Buffalo Meatballs … 50
32. Beef Chuck and Barley Stew … 36	67. Chicken and kales … 51
33. Chicken, Broccoli, and Rice … 36	68. Beef, Beans, and Bananas … 51
34. Homemade Doggie Steak and Liver … 36	69. Orange Chicken … 52
35. Chicken Cake for Dogs … 37	70. Shrimp and Tuna … 52
36. Beef with Pumpkin … 37	71. Fish Pate … 52
37. Steak and Broccoli … 38	72. Cranberry Beef … 53
38. Chicken and Rice … 38	73. Turkey Gravy … 53
39. Rice and Green beans … 38	74. Ground Beef and Macaroni … 54
40. Doggie Meatballs … 38	75. Cheesy Beef Meal … 54
41. Simple Chicken & Pasta … 39	76. Wallace Braveheart's Chicken Meatloaf … 55
42. Doggie Salmon Balls … 39	77. Doggie Meaty … 55
43. Beef with Apples … 40	78. Millet Meal … 56
44. Salmon and Spinach Hash … 40	79. Mashed Butternut Squash … 56
45. Shepherd's Pie … 40	80. Chickpea Stew … 57
46. Rice and Salmon … 41	81. Dehydrated Chicken Liver … 57
47. Lentils … 41	82. Chicken Jerky … 57
48. Quinoa and Kale … 42	83. Chicken & Sweet Potato … 58
49. Rice and Minced Chicken Meal … 42	84. Turmeric Beef … 58
50. Food Pucks … 43	85. Tuna Balls … 58
51. Mixed Meat Meal … 43	86. Delicious Chicken Meal … 58
52. Chicken Casserole … 44	87. Spaghetti Squash with Veggies … 59
53. White Meat Mix … 44	88. Stir Fry Beef Meal … 59
54. Beef & Rice … 45	89. Chicken & Oats … 59
55. The Scooby Stew … 45	90. Sweet Potatoes Meal … 60
56. Meat cakes … 46	91. Strips of Dried Beef … 60
57. Scrambled Spinach and Salmon … 46	92. Chicken Gravy … 60
58. Woof Loaf … 47	93. Eggshell Dog Meal … 61
59. Chicken, Peas, And Eggs … 47	

SIDE DISHES … 62

94. Cheesy Eggs and Rice … 63	102. Fish and Peanut Cookies … 66
95. Vegetable Fish Patties … 63	103. Dried Beet Chips … 66
96. Green Eggs & Beef … 63	104. Fruit Parfait … 67
97. Italian Spinach Balls … 64	105. Healthy Homemade Strips for Dogs … 67
98. Bites of Anchovy … 64	106. Bacon Bites … 67
99. Hearty Potato … 65	107. Kiwi and Canine Kale … 68
100. Vegetable side dish … 65	108. Easter Carrot Cookies … 68
101. Pumpkin Cookies … 66	109. Sweet Potato Potstickers … 69

110. Cheerios and Peanut Butter Balls 69
111. Hot Chili 69
112. Casserole Slices 70
113. Crunchy Snacks 70
114. Potato Chicken Side Dish 71
115. Sage Chicken & Sweet Potato 71
116. Salmon Medley 71
117. Chicken, Apple, Leafy Medley 71
118. Carrot Cookies 72
119. Simple Crispy Cheese 72
120. Kale Chips 72
121. Chicken Risotto 73
122. Kale Nachos 73
123. Deli Turkey Rollups 73

TREATS 74

124. Caribbean Canine Coolers 75
125. Frozen Fruit Popsicles 75
126. Watermelon Slush 75
127. Pumpkin Ice Cream 75
128. Cream Cheese Icing 76
129. Cheese Training Treats 76
130. Pumpkin Peanut Butter Homemade Dog Treats 77
131. Mashed Potato Icing 77
132. Sorbet de Mango 77
133. Peanut Butter and Banana Dog Ice Cream 78
134. Pumpkin Treats 78
135. Cheesy Biscuits 78
136. Blueberry Fruit Rollups 78
137. Dog Ice Cream 79
138. Peanut Butter & Carob Swirl 79
139. Bacon Cookies 79
140. Carob Dog Biscuits 79
141. Basic Dog Biscuits 80
142. Popsicles with Blueberries 80
143. Banana Ice Cubes 80
144. Raw Nuggets 80
145. Homemade blackberry biscuits 81
146. Homemade Doggie Pops 81
147. Frozen Peanut Butter Banana Treats 81
148. Bacon Peanut Butter Biscuits 82
149. Basic Baked Chicken Treats 82
150. Raw Vegetable Cupcakes 82
151. Pumpkin & Peanut Butter Rounds 83
152. Raw Crunchy Treats 83
153. Crouton Treats 84
154. Carrot Cake Crunch Biscuits 84
155. Gluten-free dog treat 85
156. Banana Frozen Yogurt Treats 85

CHAPTER 7: SHOPPING LIST 86
CONCLUSION 87
RECIPES INDEX 88
REFERENCES 91

Introduction

Many pet owners are unsure whether their dog will thrive on a diet that excludes all meat or includes grains and other plant-based foods. Dog owners may be perplexed by the amount of contradictory information available regarding their dog's health requirements. You'll be relieved to learn that your dog is an omnivore, meaning they eat both plant and animal food.

This book is especially beneficial for dog owners seeking healthy alternatives to commercial dog foods. Many pet owners want to feed their dogs a nutritious specialty diet. This cookbook includes recipes for any type of diet your dog requires, from grain-free to Paleo to raw to traditional. You can closely monitor what your dog eats when you prepare food at home, which is especially beneficial for puppies and senior dogs. You may decide that preparing your dog's food is the best option for his or her overall health. This book will introduce you to a variety of nutritious foods that you can proudly serve to your four-legged friends. You will allow them to enjoy their food and treats while remaining healthy.

Homemade dog food is without a doubt the best. To provide the best nutrition for your dog, you must be able to prepare fresh homemade food. You also have control over what goes into the food and your dog's mouth.

Some dogs have digestive issues, so you'll need to try a variety of foods and preparation methods to figure out which one is best for them. Preparing your dog's food ensures that you don't get any artificial vitamins or ingredients that can be harmful to your dog.

Purchasing and preparing your own food almost always results in higher-quality meals. When you do this, you'll always know where your meat comes from and how fresh it is. Consider using organic and grass-fed beef in your homemade dog food recipes, but don't feel bad if you can't afford it; the most important thing is that you care about what your dog eats.

When you cook for your dog, you know exactly what is going into its body. This makes it easier to identify potential issues and adjust ingredients to meet their specific nutritional requirements.

There will be no more running out of dog food and having to rush out to the pet store before they close now that you've decided to become a home chef for your dog. Home-cooked meals are just another way to provide the best for them. Don't be concerned if cooking for your dog sounds like a lot of work. Just like preparing meals for yourself or your family, you'll quickly get into a routine and be able to whip up simple recipes with minimal effort. Once you've determined which ingredients are boosting your dog's performance, you can modify other recipes in the book to include more powerful ingredients. The recipes are intended to give you the flexibility to fit cooking for your dog into your life in the way that works best for you. This book will provide you with all of the information you need to get started making your own homemade dog food. It will alleviate your concerns about feeding your cherished pet. A homemade dog food diet has numerous health benefits for your dog. This is why, if done correctly, switching from commercial dog food to homemade food will be beneficial. In this book, you will also learn which ingredients to use and which to avoid to make your dog's food as healthy as possible. There will also be 50 homemade dog food recipes available here to get you started.

Let's get started.

Chapter 1: What Is a Homemade Dog Food Diet?

The term "homemade dog food" refers to food prepared at home for dogs using ingredients that we humans consume daily. Dogs on a homemade dog food diet can avoid packaged wet dog food, dry kibble, and other processed dog food products. Pet owners can choose the ingredients in their dogs' food using this diet. Because of the control over the food ingredients, there is no need to worry about dog food recalls, which is one of the reasons homemade diets are becoming increasingly popular.

Given all of the controversy surrounding the pet food market, it is understandable that more dog owners are attempting to avoid feeding their dogs commercial food products and shift to homemade dog food diets to provide their dogs with nutritious and healthy meals.

Dog parents have begun to feed their dogs homemade food for a variety of reasons, including specific health needs, more appealing and delicious meals, food allergies, and a desire to know the exact ingredients in their dogs' food. Preparing dog food and treats from human foods takes more time and effort, but many people believe it is well worth the extra effort to ensure that their dogs' food is safe and contains the high-quality ingredients they want their dogs to consume.

A pet fed a homemade diet is less likely to consume processed commercial foods like dry kibble, dehydrated food, or canned wet food.

In recent years, there has been a lot more debate about the commercial pet food industry. There have been nearly constant recalls and diet trends, both good and bad. This is why, to provide their pet with a healthy alternative, more people are avoiding commercial pet food and opting for a homemade option. However, preparing a homemade meal for your pet is a little more complicated than simply combining ingredients.

When it comes to variety, providing whole food options makes sense. As previously stated, there are numerous reasons why you might want to make your own pet food. The most important of these reasons is gaining control over your pet's diet.

Chapter 2:
The Benefits of Homemade Dog Food Diet

There are several different reasons people choose to prepare food for their dogs rather than purchase pre-packaged foods.

Health Reasons

Some dogs require special diets due to health reasons. Some people find it better to make their dog food to provide the right nutrients for their pooch.

When homemade dog food is made properly so that it's nutritionally balanced, your dog will reap all of those incredible benefits. You can't or shouldn't always trust what the label says.

Variety

Who wants to eat the same meal every day? It is, unfortunately, a sad reality for many pets. Too often, pet owners find a brand and flavor that their pet enjoys and feed it to them for the rest of their lives. How drab and monotonous. Dogs, and any other animal for that matter, crave variety just like we do. We try to mix things up when we make homemade dog food so that they get all of the nutrition they need. Having control over your dog's food allows you to diversify their daily diet. They'll appreciate it, believe me. There are numerous ways to prepare delicious meals.

You'll probably end up feeding the same kibble for at least a month if you feed a commercial dog food diet. This can become tedious for your pet and reduce its nutritional value. With a homemade dog food recipe, you can change up the ingredients regularly to provide your pet with a broader range of nutrients. The more diverse the nutrient sources in your pet's diet, the healthier they will be overall.

Eliminate Allergens

If your pet has a sensitive stomach or another type of allergy, getting a diet free of allergens may not be enough. Dog food can be easily exposed to allergens during the manufacturing process, or it can contain different allergens, such as chicken and chicken fat. When you make homemade pet food, you can control the exact ingredients and how they are prepared, allowing you to eliminate all allergens. You can consult a veterinarian or a nutritionist to find healthy alternatives.

While these are just a few of the many advantages of a homemade dog food diet, they are not without drawbacks. Consider some of the disadvantages of making your own pet food diet.

Dogs, like humans, can suffer from allergies. Unfortunately, it is frequently something in their diet that causes the allergy. Managing your dog's diet gives you the flexibility you need to ensure they get delicious food without experiencing allergy symptoms.

Knowing What They're Truly Eating

I like to know what my animals are eating. It really helps diagnose any issues. You can read a label a hundred times over, and you can still not know everything that is in the bag or can.

Regulating Food Quality

Pet food recalls are becoming more common, which may cause you to be concerned about the quality and safety of your dog's food. Making your own pet food diet allows you to control what goes into your pet's diet more than a commercial dog food diet does. Rather than simply choosing between meat and by-product, consider the cut of meat, where it comes from, and the overall quality of the meat. When it comes to pet food, you'll notice that preservatives are used. Not all preservatives are the same, and some can be harmful over time. There are methods for preserving fresh dog food without using harmful or unnecessary chemicals.

Eliminating Filler Ingredients

To bulk up their foods, many commercial pet foods will use cheap filler ingredients. These filler materials frequently lack nutritional value. This enables businesses to produce large quantities of food at a lower cost. However, these ingredients frequently pass through a pet's system, resulting in more waste. Furthermore, filler ingredients are frequently the source of allergies. You can increase the nutritional value of your pet's food by eliminating fillers and potential food allergies when you make your own homemade dog food.

Fresh, Not Preserved Food

Even the highest quality pet foods on the market contain artificial preservatives and added salts to keep the food fresh from the manufacturing plant to your home. These preservatives will not be present in homemade dog food because everything is made fresh. Preservatives frequently aggravate pre-existing health conditions, such as heart disease, leading to overall poor health. It is healthier to eat fewer preservatives and more fresh food, just as it is with humans.

A Potentially Cheaper Option

Certain pet foods, such as prescription diets or those with a distinct nutritional composition, frequently have higher manufacturing costs. This means that the cost is passed on to the pet owner, and these foods can be costly. Depending on the commercial diet you are feeding your pet, you may discover that making your own pet food is less expensive. If you are simply feeding a generic diet, however, making a homemade diet may be more expensive. You must think about and break down the individual monthly costs.

Less Waste

You will be able to use more dog-friendly leftovers from your human meals if you make your own dog food. This lowers your household's food costs as well as food waste. You can even plan your family's meals ahead of time to save money and time on pet food preparation. Bulk protein sources, fruits, and vegetables will be available. You can use leftovers for homemade dog food as long as they are dog-safe and dog-friendly. Why would you throw them away?

Nutritional Value

If you follow the nutritional guidelines, your dog will be happier and healthier with what you prepare. Making homemade dog food allows you to control their nutritional requirements. You have the freedom and knowledge to decide whether your dog needs a high-protein diet or a low-carb diet. While ingredient labels can be helpful, many commercial dog food labels are very cryptic when it comes to specifics. This means you're feeding your pet unknown and, in some cases, artificial ingredients. You will be able to use whole foods and healthy ingredients when feeding a homemade pet food diet. You will also be able to avoid feeding questionable ingredients such as by-products.

Chapter 3: Guidelines to Feed Your Dog

How Much Should My Dog Eat?

Obesity is a problem in the dog world, just as it is in humans. What's the reason? Most dog owners overfeed their pets. Feeding instructions on commercial food bags are just that: instructions. They are written for adult dogs who are not neutered; spayed and neutered dogs have lower metabolic rates and require slightly less food. Furthermore, many pet parents do not measure their dog's portions, instead simply filling the plate or (worse) "free feeding" with a bowl full of food that the dog is free to eat at any time of day.

In general, an adult dog will consume 2.5% of her body weight in raw or fresh dog food per day; large dogs consume less, while small dogs consume slightly more. If your adult dog weighs around 31 kg, it will need to eat 0.9 kg of fresh food per day or nearly 2 lb. That number will vary, sometimes significantly, depending on whether the dog is younger or older, and whether it is less or more active.

Perhaps your dog is a working dog who spends every day with you in the fields, or she is a high-energy breed that requires a lot of exercise. How much food should she consume if she is an active dog? An active dog should consume at least 3% of her body weight more food than an average dog. You can also feed your dog a higher-calorie meal to meet this requirement.

Instead, measure out your dog's food for twice-daily feedings. (Feed puppies three to four times per day.) The general rule is that your dog should consume about 2.5 percent of his body weight per day. Depending on your dog's activity level and whether you're trying to maintain, trim, or gain weight, you'll adjust this up or down. That equates to about 2.5 pounds of food per day, or 1.25 pounds of food per meal, for a 100-pound dog.

Breed/Average Weight	Daily Serving
Chihuahua/6 pounds	.15 pound per day
Shetland Sheepdog/20 pounds	.5 pound per day
Dachshund/20–25 pounds	.5–.625 pound per day
Beagle/25 pounds	.625 pound per day
Poodle/45–70 pounds	1.125–1.75 pounds per day
Bulldog/50 pounds	1.25 pounds per day
Golden Retriever/60–80 pounds	1.5–2 pounds per day
Labrador Retriever/75 pounds	1.875 pounds per day
German Shepherd/75–95 pounds	1.875–2.25 pounds per day
Greyhound/80 pounds	2 pounds per day
Rottweiler/90–110 pounds	2.25–2.75 pounds per day
Great Dane/120 pounds	3 pounds per day

Of course, this is a broad guideline that varies depending on the food you're feeding, your dog's activity level, age, and any relevant medical conditions. (If your dog is going to be outside hiking with you in cold weather, he'll need more food; if your dog is pregnant, she'll need more food.) This table provides a general baseline to start from, and you can work from there as you see if your dog is still hungry after the meal or if your dog is gaining/losing weight.

You'd think that feeding your dog would be the easiest part of your dog-owner duties. Again, incorrect! You'll need to make some decisions, which may necessitate some research.

The proper feeding of your dog is critical for obvious reasons. Overfeeding puts your pet at risk of obesity and other serious health problems. Underfeeding results in a problem dog who chews on toys, books, etc., steals food from the counter or table and is constantly in the garbage.

How often should you give your dog food?

The next step... Feeding can be scheduled or unscheduled. Free feeding entails leaving food in the puppy's bowl at all times and allowing him/her to eat whenever they are hungry. There are various schools of thought on free feeding. Some veterinarians believe that this is the best option for your puppy because they grow quickly and may need more food one day than the next. Others advise feeding your puppy four times per day.

If you have other pets, free feeding your dog can be difficult. (Try to keep the other pets away from it). When your puppy reaches the age of one year, you'll need to retrain him to eat only once or twice a day. If you continue to free-feed your dog into adulthood, you are setting the stage for an overweight dog and potentially serious health problems.

Having said that, my recommendation is to feed your puppy 4–6 times per day. They're small and full of energy. They must eat frequently to fuel their growing bodies and mature properly. Maintain a consistent feeding schedule and leave food available for 15–20 minutes. Then remove it. If your puppy is hungry, he will eat; if not, he will have another chance in a few hours. Reduce feedings to 1–2 times per day as you get older.

Chapter 4: Nutritional Guidelines

Your canine companion requires a balanced diet for optimal health and welfare, just as we humans do. With the right nutrition, your dog can grow and develop to its full potential, giving him the energy and excitement to engage in both physical and mental activities. Your dog's dietary habits may affect both his behavior and health. There is a direct link between better behavior and a biologically appropriate, well-balanced diet. By lowering his stress levels, a balanced diet of high-quality foods can help your dog feel less stressed and more at ease. If you give your dog the nutrition he needs, he will be less likely to develop bad habits. The quality of the source of the essential nutrients required by a dog is also important. A well-balanced, nutritious canine diet should only contain premium ingredients; it should not contain extraneous ingredients such as food coloring, unidentified animal byproducts, or chemical preservatives. The majority of animal nutritionists agree with this.

Dogs' energy requirements may vary depending on a variety of factors. It is critical to meet your dog's specific energy needs to support its daily lifestyle. Some of the contributing factors are growth, reproduction (unaltered vs altered), adult age groups (young, middle, and older), activity level, breed, and medical and behavioral issues.

The majority of the energy in the diet comes from fats and proteins, with carbs coming in second. A diet's caloric content determines the quality of the food and the recommended daily calorie intake. Your dog's daily energy requirements should be met by the food. All nutrients must be balanced for optimal absorption by the body and appropriate utilization by each biological system. Your dog's digestive system will be unable to physically ingest enough of the diet if it lacks sufficient energy, and it will be unable to obtain the nutrients required.

Dogs on an energy-rich diet, for example, will consume less food overall. In this case, it is critical to ensure that the percentage of other vital nutrients consumed is sufficient to compensate for the lower volume consumed. A feeding study is the only way to determine whether a meal has enough energy to ensure that the ingredients are sufficient to maintain a healthy everyday life.

Essential Nutrients

Proteins

Proteins are required for the formation and maintenance of cartilage, tendons, and ligaments. Furthermore, protein in dog food aids in the production of blood, muscle, skin, hair, and nails. When protein is broken down, amino acids are produced, which are vital nutrients for dogs. Amino acids are required by dogs' bodies to produce energy and maintain life. Dogs require ten essential amino acids to live a healthy life. Because the body is unable to produce these nutrients, they must be obtained through diet.

To prevent and treat specific diseases, veterinary nutritionists disagree on whether to feed a high-protein or low-protein diet. Low-protein diets may be recommended for some conditions to reduce ammonia levels in the body. Ammonia is produced as a byproduct of protein breakdown and is toxic to tissue and cells. Although ammonia is produced throughout the body, the liver and kidneys contain 90% of it. Reduced intake of non-essential amino acids and total protein can help to relieve the strain on these organs. If you are considering feeding your dog a protein-specific diet due to their condition, consult with your veterinarian or a board-certified veterinary nutritionist first.

Carbohydrates

Carbohydrates play an important role in a dog's diet by providing energy. Carbohydrates are essential to a dog's daily diet because they provide dietary fiber as well as energy in the form of glucose. If the body cannot obtain glucose from carbohydrates, it will divert amino acids from other bodily functions.

Furthermore, carbohydrates generate heat within the body, serve as the foundation for additional nutrition, and have the potential to become fat. (Some carbohydrates). Dogs and growing animals should be fed a diet containing at least 20% carbohydrates.

Carbohydrate-derived fiber

Fiber, a type of carbohydrate, is essential for a dog's digestive system to function properly. It helps to keep the colon healthy by working with the bacteria in the gut. The fiber measurement is provided as crude fiber. (The insoluble portions). Total dietary fiber is made up of both soluble and insoluble fibers.

Fats

Fats are solid lipids composed primarily of triglycerides at room temperature. Dietary fat is the most concentrated source of energy in pet food. (2.25 times more calories than proteins or carbohydrates). Fat is used by the body for a variety of purposes, including energy production and the absorption of fat-soluble vitamins. One of the most important tasks is to provide the necessary fatty acids. (EFAs). EFAs help dogs maintain healthy skin and coat quality while also reducing cellular inflammation. The polyunsaturated fatty acids omega-3 and omega-6 are both important.

A lack of fatty acids may aggravate some dermatological diseases, slow wound healing, and result in dull, lifeless hair. High-fat diets can increase the risk of obesity and necessitate more vitamin E supplementation because vitamin E is involved in antioxidant protection. For fat-soluble vitamins to be absorbed, 1% to 2% of the food must contain fat.

Your veterinarian may recommend omega-3 fatty acids to help reduce inflammation caused by conditions such as arthritis, some cancers, burns, dermatitis, inflammatory bowel disease, and kidney disease. Omega-3 fatty acids play an important role in the health and functionality of cartilage. Marine fish oils, flaxseed oils, and canola oils all contain omega-3 fatty acids.

Water

Water is regarded as the most important nutrient because it serves so many important functions, including

- Temperature regulation
- Sorting proteins, carbohydrates, and fats
- Giving the body shape and structure
- Maintaining the shape of the eye
- Lubrication of joints
- Keeping the nervous system safe
- Water is provided for dogs by both their diet and their water consumption.

A healthy, well-adjusted dog requires 2.5 times the amount of water they consume in dry matter per day. Another way to consider how much water a dog requires each day is that it should be equal to the amount of energy (or food content) consumed. This is determined by the amount of dry matter ingested as well as many other factors that affect the body. (Such as age, gender, size, stress, etc.).

A dog on a wet diet will typically drink less water throughout the day (by more than 75% less) due to the higher moisture content. Water should be available to dogs at all times. It's critical to monitor their daily food intake and notify your veterinarian if it rises or falls.

Vitamins

Vitamins are a diverse and complicated topic. Numerous vitamins serve a variety of functions in the body of a dog. DNA replication, bone development, blood clotting, normal eye function, and neurological function are among these functions. A nutrient must have five characteristics to be classified as a vitamin:

1. The nutrient must take the form of an organic compound that is not fat, carbohydrate, or protein.
2. It should be a required dietary component.
3. It must be present in trace amounts for the body to function normally.
4. Its absence will result in a deficiency or a reduction in normal body functions.
5. It cannot be synthesized naturally in sufficient quantities in the body for normal body function.

You should closely monitor the vitamin sources in your dog's diet because deficiencies and excesses can occur due to inconsistencies in natural food products such as liver and lungs. It may be preferable to use a vitamin and mineral supplement to ensure proper amounts.

Vitamins are used by the body of a dog for a variety of purposes, including DNA synthesis, bone formation, blood coagulation, normal eye function, and neurologic function.

- To be classified as a vitamin, a nutrient must possess the following five characteristics:
- The nutrient must be a non-protein, carbohydrate, or fat organic substance.
- It is an essential component of the diet.
- Only a small amount is required for normal function.
- Absence causes a deficit or reduces normal functioning.
- It cannot be produced in sufficient quantities by the body to support normal function.

Overdosing on vitamins and other nutrients can result in toxicity and other complications. Because multiple vitamins are occasionally required to complete a reaction, vitamin deficiencies have the potential to cascade. Because natural food items vary, it's critical to keep an eye on the sources of vitamins in a dog's diet to avoid deficiencies and overdoses. (Liver, lungs). It may be preferable to take a vitamin and mineral supplement to ensure adequate levels.

Chapter 5: Prohibited Foods

Raisins and grapes

Since raisins are dried grapes, it stands to reason that both are on the list. They have the potential to cause severe kidney failure. There are several possibilities as to what is causing it. Salicylate, an aspirin-like drug found in grapes, may be causing a reduction in blood flow to the kidneys. Other researchers suspect it is a mycotoxin, which is a toxic substance produced by mold or fungi.

Some dogs develop clinical signs of acute renal failure within 48 hours of consuming what appears to be a small number of raisins or grapes.

Cherries

The pits, leaves, and stems of cherries are poisonous because they contain cyanide. Every now and then, a couple of cherries that have been seeded and de-stemmed are fine. Not too many and not too frequently. There are no seeds, stems, or leaves.

Nightshade

Any member of the Nightshade family, such as tomatoes or eggplant. Potatoes are also members of the Nightshade family, but as long as they are cooked, they are safe for your dog to consume.

Avocado

This is similar to a cherry. The danger comes from eating the avocado plant's pit, skin, leaves, or bark. However, I've heard that the fruit can also make them sick.

Avocados contain persin, which can cause diarrhea, vomiting, and damage to the heart muscle. The pit of an avocado is the most dangerous part because it is a choking hazard and contains a lot of persin.

If you suspect your dog has eaten an avocado pit, contact your veterinarian right away. If your dog ate a small slice of avocado, it should be fine, but keep an eye on him and contact your veterinarian if necessary.

Mushrooms

Mushrooms that are safe for human consumption can usually be eaten by dogs. However, in the wild, they should avoid eating any random mushrooms that cannot be positively identified as safe.

Rhubarb Leaf

Rhubarb leaves are poisonous. The stems are not poisonous and can be beneficial to constipated dogs.

Macadamia

In small amounts, macadamia nuts can be toxic. The side effects are usually mild and can be managed at home, but this is not always the case. If your dog consumes any of these nuts, look for symptoms such as weakness in the back legs, diarrhea, and vomiting. You should contact your veterinarian. Even small amounts of macadamia nuts can be fatal to your dog. Symptoms include muscle shaking, vomiting, a high fever, and weakness in the back legs. If your dog eats chocolate that contains macadamia nuts, the symptoms may be severe.

Xylitol

This artificial sweetener elevates insulin levels, resulting in severe hypoglycemia.

Nutmeg

Nutmeg is toxic to dogs. It is unquestionably a NO. Too much nutmeg can also be toxic to humans. Myristicin, which is found in nutmeg, is a natural insecticide.

Chocolate

It is not advisable to feed chocolate to pets. Chocolate contains theobromine, a chemical related to caffeine. Because theobromine is not quickly digested, the dog is especially sensitive to even a small dose. Theobromine has a half-life of 6 hours in humans but 17.5 hours in dogs. Theobromine is found in chocolate. In small amounts, your dog will most likely have an upset stomach. Tremors, seizures, internal bleeding, irregular heartbeat, and heart attack can all occur in large doses of theobromine. Because of artificial sweeteners like xylitol, sugar-free chocolate can be even more problematic.

Garlic and onions

Onions contain n-propyl disulfide, which may harm the lipid membranes of red blood cells if consumed. This membrane damage causes hemoglobin to become permanently denatured, and Heinz bodies are formed in red blood cells. The result is Heinz's anemia, a condition in which red blood cells are damaged. While garlic may be beneficial to dogs in small doses, excessive amounts can be harmful. Garlic is related to onions, which are harmful to dogs because they destroy their red blood cell levels, resulting in anemia. Weakness, vomiting, and breathing difficulties are all possible symptoms.

Alcohol

Do not purposefully give your dog alcohol. Alcohol can cause not only intoxication, loss of coordination, weak breathing, and abnormal acidity, but also coma or death. Find out what dogs can safely drink. This includes rubbing alcohol and hand sanitizers containing alcohol. When ingested or licked off the paws in large quantities, alcohol-based hand sanitizers can cause stomach problems such as vomiting or, if the alcohol level is high enough, alcohol poisoning.

Yeast dough

If consumed raw, this may ferment in your dog's stomach. The fermentation may cause alcohol poisoning, and the rise may cause stomach pain in your pup.

Chapter 6:
Making Your Own Dog Food

1. Berry Oatmeal & Pumpkin

Preparation Time: 10 Minutes
Cooking Time: 30 Minutes
Serving: Poodle
Ingredients:
- 2 cups steel-cut oats
- ¼ cup pumpkin puree
- ¼ cup blueberries
- ¼ cup chopped spinach

Directions:
1. Cook the oats until it is soft
2. Chop the blueberries and spinach
3. Mix all the ingredients together
4. Finally, serve

Nutrition: Calories: 273; Fat: 2 g; Net Carbs: 51 g; Protein: 7g

2. Sweet Potato & Peanut Butter

Preparation Time: 10 Minutes
Cooking Time: 30 Minutes
Serving: Beagle
Ingredients:
- 4 sweet potatoes
- 1 cup white rice
- 1 cup all-natural peanut butter
- 1 apple, peeled and diced
- ½ cup carrots

Directions:
1. Cook rice until it is very soft
2. Prick sweet potato and microwave for just 10 minutes until it is soft
3. Steam carrots and chop them
4. Microwave peanut butter to soften it up
5. Mix them all together

Nutrition: Calories: 210; Fat: 7 g; Net Carbs: 28 g; Protein: 7g

3. Peanut Butter Mix

Preparation Time: 10 Minutes
Cooking Time: 30 Minutes
Serving: Dachshund
Ingredients:
- 1 cup all-natural peanut butter
- 2 tbsp coconut oil
- 3 pounds turkey
- 1 cup carrots
- ½ cup spinach
- 1 cup celery

Directions:
1. Cook the turkey properly
2. Steam the carrots and celery and then chop them
3. Chop the spinach into tiny bits
4. Mix all ingredients together and serve

Nutrition: Calories: 160; Fat: 4 g; Net Carbs: 33 g; Protein: 9g

4. Deviled eggs

Preparation Time: 10 Minutes
Cooking Time: 30 Minutes
Serving: Dachshund
Ingredients:

- 6 large eggs
- 2 tbsp yellow mustard
- A pinch sea salt
- 2–3 tbsp mayonnaise
- A pinch red pepper

Directions:

1. Get yourself a pot. Pour some water into the container and add the eggs. Cook the eggs for a few minutes.
2. Get yourself a bowl. Fill it with cold water.
3. Remove the eggs and place them in the bowl after five minutes.
4. Allow the eggs to cool. When necessary, you can replace the water.
5. When the eggs are cool enough to handle, carefully peel them.
6. Divide the eggs in half, then remove the yolks and set them aside.
7. Combine the mayonnaise, mustard, and salt in a mixing bowl. Then, using a spoon, thoroughly combine everything.
8. When you're finished, grab a piping bag. Fill a bag with the mixture and pipe it into the egg whites.
9. Sprinkle some pepper on top of the eggs.

Nutrition: Calories: 196; Fat: 16.8 g; Net Carbs: 5.7 g; Protein: 6.7 g

5. Mini Liver Quiche

Preparation Time: 10 Minutes
Cooking Time: 30 Minutes
Serving: Shetland Sheepdog
Ingredients:

- All-purpose flour (750 ml)
- Unsalted butter (½ cup)
- 250 ml unsweetened milk
- Salt (a pinch)
- 5 eggs (large)
- 1 cup mashed liver
- 2 tbsp Fresh chives
- 1 small cup shred cheese
- 3 pieces bacon

Directions:

1. Preheat your oven to 350°F.
2. Combine the flour, butter, milk, salt, and two eggs in a clean, dry bowl. Combine thoroughly.
3. Grease a muffin tin with oil, then spoon the dough into each hole. To make the crust, press the combined dough. Repeat for the remaining holes.
4. Sprinkle the chives and bacon into each hole, then pour in the cheese.
5. In a separate bowl, whisk together the remaining eggs, garlic, and salt. Fill the tin almost to the top with the mixture.
6. Bake for 25 minutes, or until the filling is tender and the crust is golden brown.

Nutrition: Calories: 130; Fat: 2 g; Net Carbs: 18 g; Protein: 9 g

6. Chia Seed Oatmeal

Preparation Time: 10 Minutes
Cooking Time: 30 Minutes
Serving: Beagle
Ingredients:
- 1 cup unsweetened almond milk
- 1 cup old-fashioned oats
- 2 tbsp chia seeds
- 2 apples
- 2 tbsp raw honey
- 1 tsp lemon juice
- 1 cup low-fat plain Greek yogurt

Directions:
1. Pour almond milk over oats and chia seeds in a medium mixing bowl. Place aside.
2. Toss the apples with honey and lemon juice after peeling, coring, and grating them. (Be sure to discard apple seeds.) Combine the chia seed and oats mixture with the apples and yogurt.
3. Refrigerate overnight after thoroughly mixing. Chill for at least 12 hours to allow the chia seeds to plump up. Store in the refrigerator for up to 5 days.

Nutrition: Calories: 237.8; Fat: 16.3 g; Net Carbs: 7.1 g; Protein: 16.3 g

7. Spinach Omelet

Preparation Time: 10 Minutes
Cooking Time: 30 Minutes
Serving: Chihuahua
Ingredients:
- 2 eggs
- 1 cup baby spinach leaves, torn
- 1 tbsp grated Parmesan cheese

Directions:
1. In a small bowl, whisk together the eggs, spinach, and cheese. Pour into a nonstick skillet that has been sprayed with cooking spray.
2. Cook until partially set, about 5 minutes, then flip with a spatula to finish to the desired doneness.
3. Allow cooling before serving. Refrigerate any leftovers for up to 3 days.

Nutrition: Calories: 45; Fat: 2 g; Net Carbs: 4 g; Protein: 1 g

8. Homemade Dog French omelet

Preparation Time: 10 Minutes
Cooking Time: 30 Minutes
Serving: Labrador Retriever
Ingredients:
- 1/2 cup sliced grilled salmon fillet
- 2 eggs
- 1/2 green pepper, diced

Directions:
1. Add a few drops of olive oil.
2. Whisk the eggs before adding them to the pan.
3. Cook for a few minutes before adding the peppers and salmon.
4. Fold the egg until it is completely cooked. Allow cooling before serving after removing from the heat.

Nutrition: Calories: 428.2; Fat: 15.4 g; Net Carbs: 12.7 g; Protein: 57.7 g

9. Cottage Cheese Breakfast

Preparation Time: 10 Minutes
Cooking Time: 30 Minutes
Serving: Chihuahua
Ingredients:

- 1/3 cup cottage cheese
- 1/3 cup plain yogurt
- 1/3 cup mashed blueberries

Directions:

1. Mix all ingredients together in a medium bowl and serve. If you have a small dog and only need a portion of this dish, you can store the remainder in the refrigerator for up to 5 days.

Nutrition: Calories: 79; Fat: 4.4 g; Net Carbs: 3.3 g; Protein: 6.8g

10. Blueberry Muffin

Preparation Time: 10 Minutes
Cooking Time: 30 Minutes
Serving: Shetland Sheepdog
Ingredients:

- 1 cup rolled oats
- 1 cup whole wheat flour
- 1/2 tsp cinnamon
- 3/4 cup buttermilk
- 1 egg, slightly beaten
- 1/4 cup applesauce, unsweetened
- 1 cup frozen blueberries, rinsed and roughly chopped

Directions:

1. Set the oven to 400°F.
2. Use a flour-based nonstick spray on muffin tins.
3. Oats, flour, and cinnamon are combined in a big basin.
4. Stir together the buttermilk, egg, and applesauce in a separate medium basin.
5. The mixture of buttermilk should be added to the oat mixture.
6. Stir just until wet.
7. Combine blueberries (no need to thaw, they can go in frozen).
8. Do not fill the muffin tin, leave it half-full.
9. Bake for 15–20 minutes, or until a toothpick inserted in the center comes out clean.
10. On a wire rack, let the muffin pan cool for 5 minutes.
11. Before serving, remove from pan and allow cool fully on a wire rack.

Nutrition: Calories: 130; Fat: 9 g; Net Carbs: 2 g; Protein: 11 g

11. Carrot Cake Muffins

Preparation Time: 10 Minutes
Cooking Time: 30 Minutes
Serving: Poodle
Ingredients:
- 2 cups shredded carrots
- 3 eggs
- 1/2 cup applesauce, unsweetened
- 2 tsp cinnamon
- 1/2 cup rolled oats
- 3 cups whole wheat flour

Directions:
1. Preheat the oven to 350°F.
2. Lightly mist the muffin cups.
3. In a large mixing bowl, combine the carrots, eggs, and applesauce. Set aside.
4. In a separate medium bowl, combine the cinnamon, oats, and flour.
5. Gradually add the dry ingredients. To combine, stir everything together thoroughly.
1. Fill the muffin pan halfway with the mixture. Because the dough will be thick, you may need to moisten your fingers to push it into place.
6. Don't be concerned about overfilling the muffin tray because the dog cupcake won't rise much.
7. Bake for 25 minutes at 350°F.
8. Allow it to cool completely on a wire rack before icing or serving.

Nutrition: Calories: 284; Fat: 0.7 g; Net Carbs: 6 g; Protein: 1g

12. Meat Dog Cake

Preparation Time: 10 Minutes
Cooking Time: 30 Minutes
Serving: Beagle
Ingredients:
- 1/2 cup brown rice
- 1/2 cup frozen peas, thawed
- 1 celery stalk, roughly chopped
- 2 lb lean ground beef
- 3 eggs
- 1 1/2 Tbsp olive oil
- 1/2 cup rolled oats
- 1 medium potato, shredded, no green parts, see foods poisonous to dogs for more information
- 2 medium carrots, shredded

Directions:
1. Turn the oven on to 400°F.
2. Grease the loaf pan with cooking spray.
3. Salt and oil should not be added to the rice when it is cooked according to the directions on the box. Let cool.
4. The peas and the next 5 ingredients (through the eggs) should be combined in a big bowl and stirred together with a wooden spoon. Use your hands if necessary to completely blend.
5. Then, add cooled rice, rolled oats, and olive oil to the meat and vegetable combination.
6. In the loaf pan, spread the ingredients.
7. Fill the pans with the beef mixture and press down firmly.
8. Bake for 45 minutes.
9. On a wire rack, let cool fully.

Nutrition: Calories: 220; Fat: 8 g; Net Carbs: 3 g; Protein: 28 g

13. Mini Pumpkin Muffins

Preparation Time: 20 minutes
Cooking Time: 20 minutes
Serving: Shetland Sheepdog
Ingredients:
- Rice flour (1 2/3 cups)
- 1 tbsp baking soda
- ¼ tsp cinnamon
- 2 tbsp molasses
- 1 ¾ cup pureed pumpkin
- ½ cup canola olive oil
- 2 gently beaten eggs
- water (⅓ cup)

Directions:
1. Preheat the oven to 350°F (180°C). Grease or line a small muffin tin with parchment paper.
2. In a large mixing bowl, combine rice flour, baking soda, cinnamon, and molasses, then add pumpkin purée, oil, and eggs. As needed, add more water until the mixture resembles mashed potatoes.
3. Divide the mixture evenly among the muffin cups and bake for 20 minutes.
4. Remove from the oven and set aside to cool completely before serving or storing. In an airtight container, store for up to 5 days or freeze for up to 6 months.

Nutrition: Calories: 113; Fat: 9 g; Net Carbs: 2 g; Protein: 6g

14. Scrambled Eggs

Preparation Time: 10 Minutes
Cooking Time: 30 Minutes
Serving: Shetland Sheepdog
Ingredients:
- 1 large egg
- 1 tbsp unsalted butter

Directions:
1. Whisk the egg in a small bowl.
2. Heat the butter in a small skillet over medium-low heat.
3. Add the beaten egg to the skillet and scramble, pulling the egg toward you and folding it, until it forms soft curds and there is no liquid left in the skillet.
4. Cool the egg and serve.

Nutrition: Calories: 165; Fat: 5 g; Fiber: 6 g; Carbs: 22 g; Protein: 5 g

15. Apple Dog Cakes

Preparation Time: 10 Minutes
Cooking Time: 30 Minutes
Serving: Shetland Sheepdog
Ingredients:
- 2 cups Water
- No sugar applesauce
- 2 tbsp Honey
- 1 Egg
- 2 tbsp Vanilla extract
- 1 cup Wheat flour
- 3 Dried apple
- 2 tbsp Baking powder

Directions:
1. Preheat the oven to 350°F. In a separate bowl, combine the wet ingredients and add the extract.
2. Combine the flour, baking powder, and dried apple in the second bowl.
3. Properly combine the ingredients.
4. Grease the muffin tins and spoon the batter into them.
5. Bake the cakes until a skewer inserted into the center comes out clean.
6. Mix in the remaining ingredients until thoroughly combined. Fill each muffin cup halfway with batter.

Nutrition: Calories: 140; Fat: 7 g; Fiber: 6 g; Carbs: 22 g; Protein: 7 g

16. Homemade Turkey Omelet

Preparation Time: 10 Minutes
Cooking Time: 30 Minutes
Serving: Dachshund
Ingredients:
- 2 turkey bacon slices
- 1 egg
- ¼ Alfalfa sprouts

Directions:
1. Cook turkey bacon as directed on the box.
2. The stirred-up egg is fried over medium heat.
3. To make an omelet, place alfalfa sprouts on top of the egg and fold over.
4. Serve chilled and in bite-sized pieces.

Nutrition: Calories: 153.8; Fat: 6 g; Net Carbs: 9.4 g; Protein: 15.8 g

17. Fishermen's Eggs

Preparation Time: 10 Minutes
Cooking Time: 30 Minutes
Serving: Bulldog
Ingredients:
- 1 (3.75-ounce) can sardines in water
- 2 tbsp fresh parsley
- 4 eggs

Directions:
1. Preheat the oven to 375°F. Coat an 8" 8" oven-safe casserole dish with nonstick spray.
2. Drain sardines (reserve water for another recipe or a tasty dog food topping). Sardines should be chopped and mixed with parsley.
3. Fill the prepared dish halfway with the sardine mixture, then top with the eggs. (Either beat the eggs and pour over the sardines or crack each egg individually on a different portion of the mixture.)
4. Bake for 15 minutes, or until eggs are cooked to the desired doneness.
5. Allow cooling before serving your dog. Refrigerate for 3 days or freeze for up to 6 months in an airtight container.

Nutrition: Calories: 303.4; Fat: 26.9 g; Net Carbs: 2.1 g; Protein: 13.2 g

18. Almond and Banana Treats

Preparation Time: 10 Minutes

Cooking Time: 30 Minutes

Serving: Dachshund

Ingredients:

- 1 tsp Cinnamon
- ½ Banana banana)
- ¾ cup Almond Butter, unsalted
- 1 Egg

Directions:

1. Preheat oven to 350°F. Use parchment paper to line a baking sheet.
2. In a bowl mash the banana and add the rest of the ingredients.
3. Blend well and spoon onto the parchment paper.
4. Bake for a minimum of 10 minutes.
5. Let cool before serving.

Nutrition: Calories: 170.7; Fat: 1.7 g; Net Carbs: 6.4 g; Protein: 13.9 g

Main Dishes

19. Beef and Sweet Potato Stew

Preparation Time: 10 Minutes

Cooking Time: 30 Minutes

Serving:

Ingredients:

- 1-pound beef stew meat
- ½ cup carrots
- 1 sweet potato
- ½ cup green beans
- ½ cup flour
- ½ cup water
- 1 tbsp vegetable oil

Directions:

1. Cool the sweet potato after baking it.
2. Cook the stew meat in a skillet with vegetable oil over medium heat.
3. Cut the sweet potato into cubes.
4. Remove and set aside the beef.
5. Stir in the water and flour to the beef fat in the skillet until a gravy forms.
6. Mix in the vegetables and beef with the gravy.
7. Cook until the vegetables are soft.
8. Allow cooling before serving and store leftovers.

Nutrition: Calories: 125; Fat: 5 g; Fiber: 4 g; Carbs: 12 g; Protein: 5 g

20. Chicken Soup

Preparation Time: 10 Minutes

Cooking Time: 30 Minutes

Serving: Beagle

Ingredients:

- 3 pounds chicken necks
- 2 stalks celery diced
- A handful parsley
- 2 carrots diced
- 1 tbsp sea salt
- A dash rosemary
- A dash thyme

Directions:

1. Add all ingredients to a large soup pot.
2. Bring to a boil over high heat.
3. Remove the foam from the top and reduce heat until simmering.
4. Cook for eight hours.
5. Allow cooling overnight in the refrigerator.
6. Remove the fat from the top of the pot.
7. Strain the broth and throw away chunks.
8. Serve the broth warm and refrigerate the leftovers.

Nutrition: Calories: 240; Fat: 10 g; Net Carbs: 33 g; Protein: 5 g

21. Broccoli Beef with Barley

Preparation Time: 10 Minutes
Cooking Time: 30 Minutes
Serving: Bulldog
Ingredients:

- ½ cup ground chicken
- ½ cup stew meat
- 1 cup white rice
- ¼ cup carrots chopped
- ¼ cup broccoli chopped
- 1 tbsp corn oil
- ¼ tsp salt
- 1 tsp bone meal

Directions:

1. Cook the barley according to the package directions.
2. Chicken and beef should be diced.
3. Cook the beef and meat until they are done.
4. Carrots and broccoli should be steamed.
5. Vegetables should be mashed together.
6. Allow the ingredients to cool before mixing thoroughly.
7. Serve a portion and store any leftovers in the refrigerator.

Nutrition: Calories: 351; Fat: 27 g; Net Carbs: 18 g; Protein: 11g

22. Vegetable Bowl

Preparation Time: 10 Minutes
Cooking Time: 30 Minutes
Serving: Beagle
Ingredients:

- 1 large sweet potato
- 1 can black beans drained and rinsed
- ⅔ cups brown rice
- 1 ⅓ cup water
- 6 kale leaves

Directions:

1. Preheat the oven to 400°F.
2. Line the baking sheet with tin foil.
3. Bake sweet potatoes for one hour.
4. Cook rice according to instructions.
5. Chop sweet potato when cooled.
6. Combine ingredients and separate into three servings.
7. Serve and refrigerate leftovers.

Nutrition: Calories: 207; Fat: 15.4 g; Net Carbs: 1 g; Protein: 16.1 g

23. Max and Penny's Spinach

Preparation Time: 20 minutes
Cooking Time: 25 minutes
Serving: Bulldog
Ingredients:
- 2 large eggs
- 2 tbsp extra virgin olive oil
- 2 cups cooked brown rice
- 2 cups fresh sprouting spinach
- 1 can drained and chopped sprats (8.5oz/240g)

Directions:
1. Bring a saucepan of water to a high boil. Cook the rice according to the package directions. This should take 18–25 minutes, or until the rice is cooked and the liquid has been absorbed.
2. Using a fork, mash the eggs in a mixing cup. Cook the eggs in a skillet over medium heat until they are firm. Take the pan off the heat.
3. Remove the eggs from the pan and slice them into thin strips.
4. Heat the rice and olive oil in a skillet over medium heat. Continue to stir until the rice is heated, then add the spinach. Simmer, covered, until the spinach is tender. Mix in the sprats and eggs until thoroughly combined.
5. Set aside to cool before serving. Refrigerate for 3 days or freeze in an airtight container for up to 6 months.

Nutrition: Calories: 350; Fat: 18 g; Net Carbs: 27 g; Protein: 22g

24. Pumpkin Rice

Preparation Time: 10 minutes
Cooking Time: 20 minutes
Serving: Chihuahua
Ingredients:
- 1 tbsp olive oil
- 1 cup frozen mixed veggies (without onions and garlic)
- 1 cup pureed pumpkin
- 2 cups broth (chicken or veggie)
- 2 cups instant brown rice, uncooked

Directions:
1. In a large saucepan, bring the vegetables, Pumpkin Purée, and water to a boil. Stir once or twice while it cooks.
2. Add the rice to the saucepan and return to a boil over medium heat. Reduce the temperature to low and cook for another 5 minutes.
3. Remove from heat and set aside for 10 minutes, until the rice and veggies have absorbed all of the liquid.
4. Allow for complete cooling before serving it to your dog. Refrigerate for 3–4 days or freeze for up to 6 months in an airtight container.

Nutrition: Calories: 42; Fat: 3 g; Net Carbs: 0.6 g; Protein: 4 g

25. Tahini Fish

Preparation Time: 10 Minutes
Cooking Time: 30 Minutes
Serving: Labrador Retriever
Ingredients:
- 1 cup chopped carrots
- ½ cup tahini
- 4 pounds white fish
- 1 cup broth
- 1 can garbanzo beans
- 4 eggs

Directions:
1. Bake fish until cooked all the way through.
2. Add broth, carrots, and drained beans to a pot and heat until the carrots are soft.
3. Add tahini and stir.
4. Add eggs and cook.
5. Add everything and mix it.

Nutrition: Calories: 364; Fat: 27 g; Net Carbs: 13 g; Protein: 17 g

26. Beef Stock

Preparation Time: 10 Minutes
Cooking Time: 30 Minutes
Serving:
Ingredients:
- 2 carrots, cut into 1" pieces
- 1-pound beef stew meat
- 5 pounds beef marrow bones
- Olive oil, as needed
- 1 celery rib, cut into 1" pieces (or celery tops from several ribs)
- 2 garlic cloves
- Water, as needed

Directions:
1. Preheat the oven to 400°F.
2. Arrange carrots, stew meat, and bones in a large roasting pan. Coat the bones with olive oil. Roast for 45 minutes, turning meat and bones halfway through, or until browned.
3. In a large stockpot, combine the bones, meat, and carrots with the drippings and browned bits. Add celery and garlic, then cover with cold water to 2" above the bones.
4. Cook stock on the lowest heat setting for 4–6 hours. Remove from the heat. Remove the bones.
5. Strain the stock through cheesecloth to separate the liquid from the vegetables and meat. Save these solids for a different dish, a stuffable treat toy, or tasty toppings for your dog's food.
6. The liquid should be refrigerated. When the fat is cold, it rises to the top of the liquid. This solidified fat should be removed and discarded. Freeze the inventory. It's convenient to freeze it in 1-cup increments in plastic zip-top bags or ice cube trays. Beef stock is a tasty frozen treat that can be used in place of water or chicken broth in many dog recipes. Refrigerate for up to 3 days or freeze for up to 6 months in an airtight container.

Nutrition: Calories: 289; Fat: 12 g; Carbs: 23g; Fiber: 4 g; Protein: 5 g

27. Chicken Stew Meal

Preparation Time: 10 Minutes
Cooking Time: 30 Minutes
Serving: Shetland Sheepdog
Ingredients:
- 4 pounds chicken breast
- 1 cup barley
- 1 pound green beans
- 1-pound broccoli and cauliflower mix
- 4 cups water
- 2 tbsp olive oil

Directions:
1. Combine water and barley in a Dutch oven.
2. Add chicken and olive oil.
3. Simmer for 40 minutes.
4. Remove the chicken and let it cool.
5. Add vegetables to the Dutch oven and cook until tender.
6. Chop chicken and combine it with the rest of the ingredients.
7. Let cool and serve or store as desired.

Nutrition: Calories: 110 kcal; Fat: 5.4 g; Carbs: 14.2 g; Protein: 2.9 g

28. Turkey Jerky

Preparation Time: 20 minutes
Cooking Time: 4 hours
Serving: Shetland Sheepdog
Ingredients:
- 2 lb (900g) lean turkey ground
- 2 tbsp teriyaki sauce (optional)

Directions:
1. Preheat the oven to 200°F (95°C) or use a food dehumidifier. Prepare a baking sheet.
2. Cut the turkey into 12-inch-wide strips. (1.2 cm). Place the sheets on the baking sheet, but make sure they are not touching.
3. Turn the strips after 2 hours of baking. Allow moisture to escape by slightly opening the oven door. Bake the strips for an additional 2 hours.
4. Take the strips out of the oven and place them on a wire drying rack to cool completely.

Nutrition: Calories: 110 kcal; Fat: 5.4 g; Carbs: 14.2 g; Protein: 2.9 g

29. Tofu and Tapioca

Preparation Time: 10 Minutes
Cooking Time: 30 Minutes
Serving: Beagle
Ingredients:

- 10.5-ounce plain tofu
- 4 cups tapioca
- ¼ tsp salt
- Potassium chloride according to weight
- Calcium carbonate according to weight

Directions:

1. Cook tapioca according to instructions, adding potassium chloride and salt to the water.
2. Allow the tapioca mix to cool.
3. Finely chop the tofu and combine it with tapioca.
4. Mix in calcium carbonate.
5. Serve and refrigerate leftovers.

Nutrition: Calories: 313; Fat: 10.4 g; Net Carbs: 14.2 g; Protein: 41.5 g

30. Triple Three (Chicken, beef, salmon)

Preparation Time: 10 Minutes
Cooking Time: 30 Minutes
Serving: German Shepherd
Ingredients:

- 1-pound chicken
- 1-pound beef
- 1-pound canned salmon
- ½ pound broccoli
- ½ pound carrots
- ½ pound peas
- Eggshells are optional

Directions:

1. Cook chicken and beef until cooked thoroughly
2. Steam broccoli, carrots, and peas
3. Mix all ingredients together and serve

Nutrition: Calories: 353; Fat: 17 g; Net Carbs: 40 g; Protein: 12g

31. Pumpkin Balls

Preparation Time: 10 Minutes
Cooking Time: 30 Minutes
Serving: Rottweiler
Ingredients:

- ¼ cup plain yogurt
- ¼ cup water
- ½ cup pumpkin puree
- 1 eggshell
- 1 tbsp honey
- 1 cup coconut flour
- 1 cup quick-cooking oats
- 1 tbsp coconut oil
- 1 egg

Directions:

1. Preheat oven to 350°F.
2. Bake for 7 minutes the eggshell
3. Grind the eggshell and oats until they are a fine powder.
4. Combine all ingredients.
5. Form them into balls; these can also be made into muffins.
6. Bake for 6 minutes in the oven.

Nutrition: Calories: 526; Fat: 35 g; Net Carbs: 19 g; Protein: 37g

32. Beef Chuck and Barley Stew

Preparation Time: 10 Minutes
Cooking Time: 30 Minutes
Serving: Beagle
Ingredients:
- 3 pounds beef chuck
- 1-pound barley
- 2 pounds potatoes
- 2 pounds carrots
- ½ bunch celery
- 4 quarts water

Directions:
1. Add beef, potatoes, carrots, and celery chopped up in a stock pot.
2. Cover ingredients with water.
3. Cook on high for one hour.
4. Add the barley when the mixture is boiling.
5. Cook for 30 minutes.
6. Cool completely before serving as a meal.
7. Store rest as needed.

Nutrition: Calories: 240; Fat: 8 g; Net Carbs: 33 g; Protein: 10g

33. Chicken, Broccoli, and Rice

Preparation Time: 10 Minutes
Cooking Time: 30 Minutes
Serving: Beagle
Ingredients:
- 5 pounds diced chicken
- 5 cups cooked grain of choice
- 3 cups chopped broccoli
- 3 tbsp olive oil

Directions:
1. Cook the meat separately.
2. Add the broccoli at the end.
3. Stir and serve or store as desired.

Nutrition: Calories: 254.8; Fat: 11.1 g; Net Carbs: 33.9 g; Protein: 23 g

34. Homemade Doggie Steak and Liver

Preparation Time: 10 Minutes
Cooking Time: 30 Minutes
Serving: Bulldog
Ingredients:
- 8 pounds Ground beef
- 3 pounds Thinly sliced liver
- 4 cups rice
- 2 eggs, beaten
- 2 cups chopped mixed vegetables
- 9 cups water
- 1/4 cup rolled oats
- 2 tbsp Chopped parsley
- 1/2 cup milk
- 3 tbsp Olive oil

Directions:
1. Allow the oats, rice, and water to come to a boil.
2. Reduce the heat to low and stir in the remaining ingredients.
3. Cook for about 20 minutes or until done.
4. Fill a container halfway with the mixture.
5. After it has cooled, cut it into pieces and run. Refrigerate any remaining food in an airtight container.

Nutrition: Calories: 330; Carbs: 62 g; Fat: 6 g; Protein: 10g

35. Chicken Cake for Dogs

Preparation Time: 10 Minutes
Cooking Time: 30 Minutes
Serving: Poodle
Ingredients:

- 1 lb Chicken
- ½ cup Peas
- 1 Corn
- 1 Carrot
- 1 Apple
- 1 cup Rice
- 1 Egg

Directions:

1. Preheat the oven to 340°F.
2. Bring the chicken to a boil.
3. On the stove, cook the carrots, peas, and corn.
4. Peel the apple and carrot.
5. Cook the rice.
6. Mash the vegetables with a potato masher.
7. Place the egg in the shell and mash in the vegetables.
8. Mix thoroughly. Pour in the cooked rice.
9. Grease the cake pan, then place the cooked chicken on the bottom.
10. 2/3 of the vegetable mixture should be twisted over the chicken. Make another layer with the cooked chicken.
11. Cover the cake with the remaining vegetable mixture.
12. Bake for 35 minutes, or until thoroughly cooked. Allow cooling completely before slicing and serving.

Nutrition: Calories: 254.8; Fat: 11.1 g; Net Carbs: 33.9 g; Protein: 23 g

36. Beef with Pumpkin

Preparation Time: 10 Minutes
Cooking Time: 30 Minutes
Serving: Dachshund
Ingredients:

- 6 cups water, divided
- 2 cups brown rice
- 1 cup peas
- 1 cup chopped carrots
- 1-pound ground beef
- 2 tbsp pumpkin purée

Directions:

1. Bring 4 cups of water and the rice to a boil in a large saucepan over medium-high heat. Reduce the heat to low, cover, and simmer for 45 minutes, or until the rice is tender and the water has been absorbed.
2. Meanwhile, in a medium saucepan fitted with a steamer basket, bring the remaining 2 cups of water to a boil. Cover and steam the peas and carrots for about 10 minutes, or until tender.
3. Melt butter in a large skillet over medium-high heat. Cook until the beef is cooked through and browned for about 10 minutes.
4. Remove the beef from the skillet and drain the excess fat.
5. Stir in the cooked rice, vegetables, and pumpkin with the beef.
6. Allow cooling before serving.
7. Refrigerate leftovers in an airtight container or portioned into sealed plastic bags for up to 1 week or freeze for 3 months.

Nutrition: Calories: 165; Fat: 5 g; Fiber: 6 g; Carbs: 22 g; Protein: 5 g

37. Steak and Broccoli

Preparation Time: 10 Minutes
Cooking Time: 30 Minutes
Serving: Bulldog
Ingredients:
- 2 pieces salmon with skin
- 1 head broccoli
- 3 carrots
- 2 butternut squash
- 5 potatoes
- 2 tbsp Olive oil

Directions:
1. Tie the carrots, squash, and broccoli and simmer until cooked.
2. Shave the potatoes and bake in the oven until cooked through.
3. Cook the salmon in 1 tbsp olive oil.
4. Once everything is cooked, let it cool and mix before consuming.

Nutrition: Calories: 330; Carbs: 62 g; Fat: 6 g; Protein: 10g

38. Chicken and Rice

Preparation Time: 10 Minutes
Cooking Time: 30 Minutes
Serving: Poodle
Ingredients:
- ¼ pound cooked chicken
- 1 cup brown rice
- 1 cup peas and carrots
- 1 tbsp vegetable oil
- ¼ tsp potassium chloride

Directions:
1. Cook rice and chicken together.
2. Add vegetables last right before the meat is ready.

Nutrition: Calories: 254.8; Fat: 11.1 g; Net Carbs: 33.9 g; Protein: 23 g

39. Rice and Green beans

Preparation Time: 10 Minutes
Cooking Time: 30 Minutes
Serving: Bulldog
Ingredients:
- 1-pound turkey meat
- 1 cup cooked rice
- ½ cup green beans
- ½ cup carrots
- ¼ cup water
- 1–2 tbsp vegetable oil

Directions:
1. Cook together, adding the vegetables last. Stir until ready.

Nutrition: Calories: 320; Carbs: 45 g; Fat: 4 g; Protein: 5g

40. Doggie Meatballs

Preparation Time: 10 Minutes
Cooking Time: 30 Minutes
Serving: Bulldog
Ingredients:
- 1 cup Ground beef
- 1/2 cup seeded and seeded apples, grated
- 1/4 cup honey
- 2 tbsp omega oil
- 1 tbsp parsley flakes

Directions:
2. Mix all of the ingredients thoroughly with your hands.
3. Divide the ingredients and shape them into meatballs.
4. Bake until done in the oven or in a skillet.
5. Before serving, allow the meatballs to cool.

Nutrition: Calories: 223; Fat: 4 g; Net Carbs: 7 g; Protein: 9g

41. Simple Chicken & Pasta

Preparation Time: 10 Minutes
Cooking Time: 30 Minutes
Serving: Beagle
Ingredients:
- 10 ⅜ oz skinless, boneless chicken breast, roasted
- 5 ⅝ cups cooked, salted-free enriched spaghetti
- 15 ¾ tsp Olive oil
- ¾ cups blanched, drained, and salted frozen green peas
- 8 ¼ tsp Balance Canine Plus

Directions:
1. Preheat the oven to 400°F.
2. Butterfly the raw chicken breasts to cut their thickness in half; this will speed up the cooking time. Arrange chicken breasts with raw meat on a baking sheet lined with foil. There should be no oil at all. Roast for 20 to 30 minutes, or until the juices run clear and the internal temperature reaches at least 165°F, in a 400°F oven. Remove from oven, discard liquids, and set aside to cool. Cut the chicken into bite-sized pieces.
3. While the chicken is roasting, prepare and cook the pasta according to the package directions. Remember that the amount specified in the recipe is the cooked amount, which is roughly twice the amount of dry pasta. After cooking, drain the pasta and set it aside to cool.
4. Before cooling, boil frozen peas according to package directions.
5. Measure each ingredient according to the recipe using a kitchen scale, measuring cups, and spoons. Combine all of the ingredients in a large mixing bowl and whisk well.
6. Divide the mixture evenly among seven airtight containers. Food should only be kept in the refrigerator for three days, according to Balance.
7. Feed your dog one container every two meals.
8. One container should be moved from the freezer to the refrigerator daily so that it can thaw before being fed.

Nutrition: Calories: 243; Fat: 6.7 g; Net Carbs: 39.5 g; Protein: 5.4 g

42. Doggie Salmon Balls

Preparation Time: 8 minutes
Cooking Time: 15 minutes
Serving: Dachshund
Ingredients:
- 1 egg
- 1 tbsp olive oil
- 1 cup cooked brown rice
- 1 ½ cups cooked salmon, chopped

Directions:
1. Preheat oven to 350°F. Grease lightly on a baking sheet.
2. In a mixing bowl, mix all the ingredients. Use a melon baller or spoon to scoop the mixture and roll it into balls. Place balls on the baking sheet.
3. Bake the salmon balls for about 15 minutes. Allow the salmon balls to cool before serving them to your dog. Store in the fridge for 3–4 days or in an airtight container freeze them for up to 6 months.

Nutrition: Calories: 164; Fat: 5 g; Net Carbs: 23 g; Protein: 7 g

43. Beef with Apples

Preparation Time: 10 Minutes
Cooking Time: 30 Minutes
Serving: Shetland Sheepdog
Ingredients:

- 2 cups water
- 1 cup lentils
- 1-pound ground beef
- 2 tbsp olive oil
- 2 cups baby spinach
- 1 apple, chopped

Directions:

1. Bring the water and lentils to a boil in a large saucepan over medium-high heat. Reduce the heat to low, cover, and simmer for 20 minutes, or until the lentils are tender.
2. Meanwhile, melt the butter in a large skillet over medium-high heat. Cook until the beef is cooked through and browned for about 10 minutes.
3. Remove the beef from the skillet and drain the excess fat. Place aside.
4. In a large skillet over medium-high heat, heat the olive oil. Sauté the spinach and apple for 2 to 3 minutes, or until tender. Turn off the heat in the skillet.
5. Stir together the cooked lentils and beef with the spinach and apples.
6. Allow cooling before serving.
7. Refrigerate leftovers in an airtight container or portioned into sealed plastic bags for up to 1 week or freeze for 3 months.

Nutrition: Calories: 125; Fat: 5 g; Fiber: 4 g; Carbs: 12 g; Protein: 5 g

44. Salmon and Spinach Hash

Preparation Time: 10 Minutes
Cooking Time: 30 Minutes
Serving: Golden Retriever
Ingredients:

- 1 tsp olive oil
- 1 (7.5-ounce) can salmon, drained
- 1 cup frozen spinach, thawed
- 4 eggs

Directions:

1. Heat olive oil in a medium skillet over medium-high heat. Add salmon and spinach, stirring until completely heated.
2. Add eggs and scramble.
3. Cool before serving. Refrigerate for up to 3 days.

Nutrition: Calories: 390; Fat: 25 g; Net Carbs: 24 g; Protein: 22 g

45. Shepherd's Pie

Preparation time: 10 Minutes
Cooking Time: 30 Minutes
Serving: Dachshund
Ingredients:

- Ground beef
- 1 1/3 cups mashed potatoes
- 1/2 cup of legumes
- 1/2 cup peeled and chopped carrots
- 1/2 cup breadcrumbs
- 1/4 tsp. Ground eggshell
- 1 C. parsley
- 1/2 cup, low fat, shredded

Directions:

1. Heat your oven to 375°.
2. Combine the entire ingredients into a bowl.
3. Divide the mixture between 12 muffin cups.
4. Bake for about 15 to 30 minutes or until cooked through.
5. Let cool before serving.

Nutrition: Calories 169.4, Fat: 10.8g, Net Carbs: 6.8g, Protein: 15.2g

46. Rice and Salmon

Preparation Time: 10 Minutes
Cooking Time: 30 Minutes
Serving: Chihuahua
Ingredients:
- 30 gr brown rice
- 150 gr salmon (or sardines)
- 1 raw cow femur
- 20 gr cauliflower
- 1 pinch parsley
- 3 tbsp Sunflower oil

Directions:
1. Clean the rice and bring it to a boil in plenty of water.
2. Cut the salmon into small cubes and the cauliflower into small pieces.
3. Then sauté the salmon and vegetables, finishing with a sprinkle of parsley on top.
4. Remember that raw bones should never be cooked because they can splinter when consumed.
5. When the rice is done and the salmon and vegetables are lightly cooked, combine the raw beef femur with the rice and serve.
6. Mix in a small amount of vegetable oil and set aside to cool.

Nutrition: Calories: 40; Fat: 1.5 g; Net Carbs: 5 g; Protein: 1g

47. Lentils

Preparation Time: 10 Minutes
Cooking Time: 30 Minutes
Serving: German Shepherd
Ingredients:
- 2 cups water
- 1 cup lentils

Directions:
1. Place the water and lentils in a medium saucepan and bring to a boil. Reduce heat to low, cover, and simmer until the lentils are tender for about 20 minutes.
2. Remove the saucepan from the heat.
3. Let cool before serving.
4. Store leftovers in an airtight container in the refrigerator for up to 5 days.

Nutrition: Calories: 345; Fat: 2 g; Fiber: 3 g; Carbs: 24 g; Protein: 21 g

48. Quinoa and Kale

Preparation Time: 10 Minutes
Cooking Time: 30 Minutes
Serving: Shetland Sheepdog
Ingredients:
- 500 g Organic Free Range chicken
- 1 cup Quinoa
- 3 cups kale, chopped
- 3 handfuls Green beans
- 2 Zucchini

Directions:
1. Boil the quinoa in two cups of water, then cool and set aside.
2. Cook the chicken in a large, deep pan or wok after it has been thinly sliced.
3. After adding the chopped vegetables, continue to stir-fry.
4. Once the chicken and vegetables are heated through, add the quinoa.
5. Stir in your favorite dog food supplement (see below), then serve and enjoy!

NB: Any leftovers can be frozen into ready-to-eat meals.

Nutrition: Calories: 141.2; Fat: 5.9 g; Net Carbs: 13.3 g; Protein: 9 g

49. Rice and Minced Chicken Meal

Preparation Time: 10 Minutes
Cooking Time: 30 Minutes
Serving: Bulldog
Ingredients:
- ½ cup ground chicken
- 1 cup white rice
- ¼ cup carrots
- ¼ cup green beans
- ½ tbsp corn oil
- ¼ tsp salt
- 1 tsp bone meal

Directions:
1. Cook the rice in boiling water.
2. To the water, add corn oil and salt.
3. Cook for 15 minutes.
4. Combine the remaining ingredients.
5. Cook for 10 minutes.
6. Remove from the heat and set aside to cool.
7. Prepare a meal and save the leftovers.

Nutrition: Calories: 330 Carbs: 62 g Fat: 6 g Protein: 10 g

50. Food Pucks

Preparation Time: 10 Minutes
Cooking Time: 30 Minutes
Serving: Dachshund
Ingredients:
- 3 cups Raw grass-fed beef
- 6 entire eggs (you may use the shell too!)
- ½ tsp sea salt, grey
- ½ cup coconut oil or grass-fed tallow canine multivitamin powder
- 1 cup Bone broth
- 1 (300-gram) sweet potato
- 2 apples, all seeds removed.
- ¼ cup ground hemp, pumpkin, or flaxseed meal
- 2 calf livers or 6 chicken livers

Directions:
1. Combine the Raw Base Recipe components (including the WHOLE egg) and any additional Boosted Supplements in the jug of your powerful blender. Blend until completely smooth. Place everything in a large mixing bowl, cover, and chill.
2. In the meantime, add the Cooked Base Recipe ingredients to your Pot and cook for 15 minutes on high pressure. Alternatively, after increasing the broth to 3 cups, transfer it to a large saucepan. After bringing it to a boil, cover and simmer for 25 minutes.
3. Thaw the Cooked Base Recipe ingredients to room temperature. Transfer to the jug of a blender and blend on high until completely smooth. Transfer the mixture to the basin containing the blended Raw Base Recipe ingredients, and fold in with a large spoon.
4. Pour into tiny silicone molds or larger silicone molds if your dog is larger. After filling each mold, place it in the freezer and leave it there for 12 hours. They can be kept in the molds or transferred to a large Ziploc bag.
5. Keep the pucks in the freezer at all times. When it's time to feed, let the food defrost on the counter for an hour or overnight in the refrigerator. Remember that there is raw meat inside; wash your hands afterward.

Nutrition: Calories: 192; Fat: 13 g; Net Carbs: 15 g; Protein: 5g

51. Mixed Meat Meal

Preparation Time: 10 Minutes
Cooking Time: 30 Minutes
Serving: Bulldog
Ingredients:
- 3 pounds cooked macaroni
- 2 pounds chicken
- 1-pound ground beef
- 1-pound broccoli stalks
- 1-pound red leaf lettuce
- ½ pound chicken liver
- ½ pound beef heart
- 1 large egg white
- 4 tbsp eggshell powder
- 1 tbsp kelp meal
- 10 drops Vitamin E

Directions:
1. Cook together meat ingredients.
2. Add vegetables ten minutes before the meat is ready.

Nutrition: Calories: 340; Fat: 28 g; Net Carbs: 3 g; Protein: 17g

52. Chicken Casserole

Preparation Time: 10 Minutes
Cooking Time: 30 Minutes
Serving: Dachshund
Ingredients:

- 4 Chicken breasts
- ½ cup Carrots, chopped
- ½ cup Oats, rolled
- ½ cup, green beans, chopped
- 4 cups Chicken broth, unsalted
- ½ cup Broccoli, chopped

Directions:

1. Remove the excess amount of fat from chicken breasts before cutting them into small chunks.
2. Over medium heat, heat a non-stick skillet and cook chicken breasts until they are no longer pink.
3. In a large pot, place chicken broth, vegetables, and chicken and bring to a boil. Let simmer for about 12–15 minutes or until the carrots have become tender.
4. Let cool before serving.

Note: The leftover portion can be refrigerated for up to five days, if the chicken breasts become stuck to the skillet, try frying in a small amount of olive oil.

Nutrition: Calories: 160; Fat: 2 g; Net Carbs: 26 g; Protein: 2 g

53. White Meat Mix

Preparation Time: 10 Minutes
Cooking Time: 30 Minutes
Serving: Dachshund
Ingredients:

- 1 lb White Fish (Mackerel is a good choice)
- 2 lb Chicken & Turkey (Bone-in or add bone meal)
- ½ lb Chicken & Turkey Organ Meat (hearts and liver works well)
- 10 leaves Fresh Spinach
- 1 cup Fresh Broccoli
- 2 Slightly Boiled Eggs

Directions:

1. Cut up your meat and veggies, so they're small and safe for consumption.
2. Mix it all up and serve. If you use canned fish that contains oil, you don't necessarily have to add any extra oil to this mix.

Nutrition: Calories: 179.3; Fat: 7.7 g; Net Carbs: 13.6 g; Protein: 11.2 g

54. Beef & Rice

Preparation Time: 10 minutes
Cooking Time: 10 minutes
Serving: Chihuahua
Ingredients:

- ¼ Pound Ground Beef (the fatter, the better)
- 2 Cups of Brown or White Rice (cooked)
- 1 Hard-Boiled Egg
- 3 Pieces Wheat Bread
- 1 Tsp Bone Meal or Calcium Carbonate Powder

Directions:

1. Brown the ground beef and make sure it is fully cooked.
2. Peel the egg and chop it.
3. Tear up the bread into small pieces.
4. Toss all of the ingredients into a medium-sized bowl and mix well.
5. Serve warm or cool (some dogs without an appetite are more likely to eat warm food).

Nutrition: Calories: 70; Fat: 1 g; Net Carbs: 13 g; Protein: 3g

55. The Scooby Stew

Preparation Time: 10 Minutes
Cooking Time: 30 Minutes
Serving: Rottweiler
Ingredients:

- 2.5 glasses water
- 1 serving brown rice
- 2 cups diced sweet potatoes
- Cut each of the two large chicken breasts into six pieces.
- 2 pounds mixed frozen vegetables (peas, green beans carrots)

Directions:

1. Place the ingredients in the slow cooker in the recommended order, covering the chicken and vegetables completely.
2. It takes 5 hours on high or 8 hours on low to cook.
3. Shred the chicken and evenly incorporate it into the rice and vegetable mixture before removing it from the slow cooker.
4. Refrigerate for up to 3 days, covered, or freeze in single-serve portions.

Nutrition: Calories: 520; Fat: 16.6 g; Net Carbs: 68.8 g; Protein: 15.4 g

56. Meat cakes

Preparation Time: 10 Minutes
Cooking Time: 30 Minutes
Serving: Chihuahua
Ingredients:

- 1 ½ cups brown rice
- 1 lb Pkg Market Pantry Ground Beef
- 3 cups water
- 8 eggs
- 2 big potatoes shredded
- 1 pinch salt
- 4 big carrots shredded
- ¼ cup Olive oil
- 2 big, chopped celery stalks
- 1 ½ cups of Regular rolled oats

Directions:

1. Preheat the oven to 400°F. (205°C). Grease three large muffin pans with 36 cups each.
2. In a medium saucepan, combine rice and water. Cook for 10 minutes, uncovered, while bringing to a boil over high heat. Cover the pan and reduce the heat to low for 20 minutes. Remove from the heat, set aside for a few minutes to cool, then fluff with a fork. In a large mixing bowl, combine the potatoes, carrots, celery, eggs, and ground meat. To combine the ingredients, use a strong spoon or your hands. Rice, rolled oats, salt, and olive oil are all recommended.
3. Fill each muffin cup halfway with the meat mixture. Firmly press the meat mixture into the pan. Bake for 45 minutes, or until the top is firm. Let it cool on a rack for 10 or more minutes.
4. Invert the muffin pan over a sheet of aluminum foil to remove the meat cakes. Tap each muffin cup to release the cake. Put airtight plastic bags in the freezer or fridge.

Nutrition: Calories: 70; Fat: 3.8 g; Net Carbs: 6.1 g; Protein: 1.5 g

57. Scrambled Spinach and Salmon

Preparation Time: 10 Minutes
Cooking Time: 30 Minutes
Serving: Poodle
Ingredients:

- 1 tsp Extra virgin olive oil
- ½ can skinless, boneless salmon (3 ounces) drained
- 2 eggs
- ½ cup thawed and drained frozen chopped spinach

Directions:

1. The oil should be heated over medium heat in a small nonstick skillet.
2. Salmon and spinach are added, and they are heated all the way through.
3. For about two minutes, while stirring continuously, add the eggs and boil them through.
4. Serve in a dog bowl after letting it slightly cool.

Nutrition: Calories: 270; Fat: 27 g; Net Carbs: 8 g; Protein: 3 g

58. Woof Loaf

Preparation Time: 10 Minutes
Cooking Time: 30 Minutes
Serving: Chihuahua
Ingredients:
- 1-pound lean turkey meat
- ½ cup Oats
- ½ cup chopped carrots2 eggs
- ½ cup peas
- 3 cooked eggs, hard

Directions:
1. Set the oven to 350°F. Combine the peas, carrots, and lean ground turkey in a bowl. Both are beneficial for cats and dogs because they provide the nutrition they need for healthy digestion and strong eyes.
2. Include the eggs and oats. Stir until the dough for the bread comes together. Eggs add added protein, while oats make your pet's coat sparkle. Add half of the mixture to a loaf pan that has been lightly greased with olive oil.
3. After placing the three hard-boiled eggs in the middle of the loaf, top with the remaining ground turkey mixture. 45 minutes of baking should be done in the oven.
4. Offer your pet a slice of the cooled bread that is half an inch thick. He'll woof for several seconds! It's a good idea to cut up a piece before giving it to your cat in her feeding dish if you're feeding it to her.

Nutrition: Calories: 27; Fat: 0.6 g; Net Carbs: 4.3 g; Protein: 1.2 g

59. Chicken, Peas, And Eggs

Preparation Time: 10 Minutes
Cooking Time: 30 Minutes
Serving: Chihuahua
Ingredients:
- 1 cup chicken chopped
- 1 chopped hard-boiled egg
- 2 tbsp nonfat plain yogurt
- ¼ cup cooked brown rice
- ½ cup carrots and peas

Directions:
1. Combine cooked ingredients and mix well.
2. Allow cooling before serving.
3. Refrigerate leftovers.

Nutrition: Calories: 87; Fat: 48 g; Net Carbs: 21 g; Protein: 33g

60. Favorite gourmet meal

Preparation Time: 10 Minutes
Cooking Time: 30 Minutes
Serving: Shetland Sheepdog
Ingredients:
- Brown rice, approximately ¾ cup
- 1/4 cup chopped zucchini
- 1 cup raw chicken
- ¼ cup chopped broccoli (steamed)
- ¼ cup mashed sweet potatoes
- 1 tbsp Virgin olive oil

Directions:
1. Begin cooking the brown rice to make this dog chow. It should be cooked in a rice cooker or on the stove according to the package directions, then set aside to cool. Before adding the ground turkey to the pan, brown it in the olive oil over medium heat. This activity should take three to five minutes to complete.
2. Crush the turkey into pieces while it cooks. Combine the rice, rice, and vegetables in a large mixing bowl. Cook for another three to five minutes with this mixture. Remove the skillet from the heat and set aside to cool completely before serving your dog.

Nutrition: Calories: 114.4; Fat: 8.5 g; Net Carbs: 3 g; Protein: 6.4 g

61. Thanksgiving meal recipe

Preparation Time: 10 Minutes
Cooking Time: 30 Minutes
Serving: Greyhound
Ingredients:

- 3 pounds skinless turkey bits (light and dark meats are both ok, but not bones.)
- 1 cup oats, cooked
- 1 lb sweet potato cubes, which is usually 2 sweet potatoes
- 2 tbsp cranberry sauce, Use the homemade sauce and make sure it doesn't contain any alcohol.
- 4 tbsp turkey gravy (you can substitute olive oil) Make sure there are no onions in the gravy.

Directions:

1. Roast a turkey or use leftover turkey:
2. Make bite-sized pieces out of the cooked turkey.
3. Sweet potatoes can be roasted or boiled. Boil for 20 minutes or 45 minutes of roasting at 400°F. Both before and after cooking, you can dice them. It could take longer to cook an entire sweet potato.
4. Following the directions on the package, prepare the oatmeal. It takes between 10 and 20 minutes to prepare regular oatmeal, which is preferable to instant.
5. The turkey, oats, sweet potatoes, and cranberry sauce should all be combined. If using oil or gravy, add it now and thoroughly combine.
6. Use the gravy sparingly and check with your veterinarian to ensure that the olive oil is safe if your dog is at all susceptible to pancreatitis or other fatty-related issues.
7. Once everything has been combined, your dog will have a delicious dinner that you may share with her if you'd like, but she might prefer to keep it all to herself.

Nutrition: Calories: 357; Fat: 11 g; Net Carbs: 51 g; Protein: 11g

62. Vegetable & Turkey Delight

Preparation Time: 10 Minutes
Cooking Time: 30 Minutes
Serving: Chihuahua
Ingredients:

- 1 cup, brown rice
- 2 cups water
- 1 pear, diced
- 1 cup broccoli, florets
- 1 cup, chopped kale
- 1 cup, diced carrots
- 1 cup, cottage cheese
- 3 tbsp vegetable oil

Directions:

1. Prepare the rice on the stove and set it aside.
2. In a skillet, combine the vegetable oil and turkey. Except for the kale, add the vegetables, being careful not to overcook either the vegetables or the meat.
3. Stir in the kale and pear.
4. Add cooked rice and cook for 5 minutes more.
5. Place in a mixing bowl and stir in the cottage cheese.
6. Chill until his next meal.

Nutrition: Calories: 22; Fat: 0.7 g; Net Carbs: 3.8 g; Protein: 1.1 g

63. Gravy with Giblets

Preparation Time: 30 minutes
Cooking Time: 75 minutes
Serving: Poodle
Ingredients:

- 1 tbsp oil (vegetable)
- 1 turkey's neck and giblets
- 1 chopped celery rib
- 1 sliced carrot
- 4 cups water
- 2 quarts (liters) chicken stock
- 2–3 tbsp flour (all-purpose)

Directions:

1. Place the neck and gizzards in a large saucepan over medium heat. Brown the meat, then add the rest of the ingredients (excluding the flour).
2. Cook for about an hour. Remove the pan from the heat.
3. Using a fine sieve, strain the broth. Fat should be skimmed off and discarded.
4. Remove the meat from the bones and discard them. Meat should be diced finely. Reheat the meat in the broth with the flour, stirring constantly. Bring to a boil, continually stirring, until the gravy thickens.
5. Remove the pan from the heat and allow it cool. Refrigerate for up to 3 days or freeze for up to 6 months in an airtight container.

Nutrition: Calories: 280; Fat: 12.2 g; Net Carbs: 30.5 g; Protein: 6.7 g

64. Beef Stew

Preparation Time: 10 Minutes
Cooking Time: 30 Minutes
Serving: Bulldog
Ingredients:

- 1 1/2 pounds beef- any kind
- ½ cup frozen peas
- ½ cup carrots
- 1 sweet potato
- 2 tbsp coconut oil
- 1 cup Water

Directions:

1. Pan-fry the beef until fully cooked & drain the oil.
2. Microwave sweet potato for 10 minutes, or until soft, after piercing it with a fork.
3. Steam the carrots and peas until they are tender.
4. Place all of the ingredients in a pot with just enough water to cover them, and cook for about 20 minutes.
5. Allow cooling before serving.

Nutrition: Calories: 287; Fat: 12 g; Carbs: 41 g; Fiber: 6 g; Protein: 8 g

65. Lamb Hash

Preparation Time: 10 Minutes
Cooking Time: 30 Minutes
Serving: Chihuahua
Ingredients:
- 2 tbsp olive oil
- 1-pound ground lamb
- 1 cup frozen mixed vegetables (without onions)
- 2 cups cooked brown rice
- 2 cups cooked white rice
- 1 cup low-fat plain yogurt

Directions:
1. In a large skillet, heat olive oil over medium-high heat. Cook lamb until no longer pink, about 10 minutes, and drain off fat.
2. Add vegetables, stirring to defrost. Remove from heat.
3. In a large bowl, combine lamb mixture, rice, and yogurt. Mix thoroughly.
4. Cool before serving.
5. Refrigerate for 3 days or freeze in an airtight container for up to 6 months.

Nutrition: Calories: 85.6; Fat: 0.5 g; Net Carbs: 17.3 g; Protein: 4.4 g

66. Buffalo Meatballs

Preparation Time: 10 Minutes
Cooking Time: 30 Minutes
Serving: Dachshund
Ingredients:
- 2 slices whole-wheat bread, cut into 1/2" cubes
- ½ cup milk
- 1 egg
- 1/3 cup grated Parmesan cheese
- 2 tbsp finely chopped parsley
- 1 pound ground bison
- 2 tbsp Olive oil, for frying

Directions:
1. Soak bread cubes in milk in a medium bowl until soft. (About 5 minutes). Remove the bread from the milk, squeeze out any excess milk, and discard the milk.
2. Combine the bread, egg, cheese, parsley, and bison in a large mixing bowl. Cut into small pieces and roll into balls.
3. Heat 12 cup olive oil in a large skillet over medium-high heat. Fry each meatball for 8–10 minutes, or until no longer pink in the center.
4. Remove from the heat and set aside to cool completely before serving. Refrigerate for 3–4 days or freeze for up to 6 months in an airtight container.

Nutrition: Calories: 185; Fat: 4.5 g; Net Carbs: 30 g; Protein: 9.1 g

67. Chicken and kales

Preparation Time: 10 Minutes
Cooking Time: 30 Minutes
Serving: Chihuahua
Ingredients:
- 4–5 cups Cooked brown rice
- 16-ounces frozen peas
- 2 entire chickens, simple, weighing around 4 pounds each
- 2 small bunches Fresh parsley leaves
- 2 chopped medium orange sweet potatoes
- 2 small to medium bunches stemmed kale
- 8 sliced whole carrots
- 8 eggs

Directions:
1. For about 1 hour and 25 minutes, or until juices run clear, roast chicken at 350°F. Cook the rice (4 cups water and 2 cups rice) and let it cool while the chickens roast.
2. Yams and carrots should be peeled, chopped, and added to a big stock pot with about ½ cup of water. Include the apple, kale, and peas. Allow to boil, then reduce heat and simmer for 30 minutes or until carrots and yams are soft. With a slotted spoon, transfer the mixture to a food processor, add the fresh parsley, and process until smooth.
3. Prepare plain scrambled eggs.
4. Chicken should be allowed to cool before being torn apart. Mix at a medium speed until the chicken is shredded. Add the eggs, vegetable puree, and cooled rice. Scoop out portions onto a prepared baking sheet with an ice cream scooper. Place portions in a freezer-safe container or bag after quickly freezing.
5. Keep enough for a day or two in the fridge to thaw before using. I microwaved frozen chunks for around 45 seconds and thawed sections for 22 seconds. Give food to your pet baby.

Nutrition: Calories: 94; Fat: 5 g; Net Carbs: 11 g; Protein: 2g

68. Beef, Beans, and Bananas

Preparation Time: 10 Minutes
Cooking Time: 30 Minutes
Serving: Shetland Sheepdog
Ingredients:
- 6 cups water, divided
- 2 cups brown rice
- 1 cup chopped green beans (about 2-inch pieces)
- 1 pound ground beef
- 1 cucumber, cut into a ½-inch dice
- 1 banana, cut into rounds

Directions:
1. Bring 4 cups of water and the rice to a boil in a large saucepan over medium-high heat. Reduce the heat to low, cover, and simmer for 45 minutes, or until the rice is tender and the water has been absorbed.
2. Meanwhile, in a medium saucepan fitted with a steamer basket, bring the remaining 2 cups of water to a boil. Cover and steam the green beans for about 15 minutes, or until tender.
3. Melt butter in a large skillet over medium-high heat. Cook until the beef is cooked through and browned for about 10 minutes.
4. Remove the beef from the skillet and drain the excess fat.
5. Stir in the cooked rice, green beans, cucumber, and banana to the beef.
6. Allow cooling before serving.
7. Refrigerate leftovers in an airtight container or portioned into sealed plastic bags for up to 1 week or freeze for 3 months.

Nutrition: Calories: 110; Fat: 5.4 g; Carbs: 14.2 g; Protein: 2.9 g

69. Orange Chicken

Preparation Time: 10 Minutes
Cooking Time: 30 Minutes
Serving: Dachshund
Ingredients:

- 1 ½ pound ground chicken
- 1 ½ tbsp bone meal
- ¼ pound broccoli
- 1 tangerine
- 1 sweet potato diced
- ¼ cup coconut oil
- ¼ pound zucchini diced
- 1 tbsp ground flaxseed
- ¼ tsp rosemary
- ¼ tsp thyme

Directions:

1. Combine meat, water, and seasonings in a soup pot and bring to a boil over medium heat.
2. Boil for 20 minutes.
3. Add fruits and vegetables and cook until tender.
4. Take off the heat and allow it to cool.
5. Stir in bone meal, flaxseed, and coconut oil.
6. Serve as a meal and store the rest.

Nutrition: Calories: 163.8; Fat: 13.9 g; Net Carbs: 1.5 g; Protein: 8.6 g

70. Shrimp and Tuna

Preparation Time: 10 Minutes
Cooking Time: 30 Minutes
Serving: Great Dane
Ingredients:

- 1 pound shrimp finely ground
- 12-ounce canned tuna
- 1 cup sweet potato mashed
- ½ cup plain yogurt
- ¼ tsp thyme
- ¼ tsp turmeric

Directions:

1. Combine all the ingredients together.
2. Form into patties.
3. Serve as a meal and store the rest.

Nutrition: Calories: 721; Fat: 289 g; Net Carbs: 15.1 g; Protein: 21.8 g

71. Fish Pate

Preparation Time: 10 Minutes
Cooking Time: 30 Minutes
Serving:
Ingredients:

- 1 can salmon
- 1 carrot
- 1 potato
- 1 egg
- 1 stalk celery
- 3 tbsp flour
- 2 tbsp Frying oil

Directions:

1. Drain and fry the salmon with the flour and egg.
2. Remove the patties from the oil.
3. Stir the veggies in the oil for five to eight minutes.
4. Mix, allow to cool, and serve.

Nutrition: Calories: 330; Carbs: 62 g; Fat: 6 g; Protein: 10g

72. Cranberry Beef

Preparation Time: 10 Minutes
Cooking Time: 30 Minutes
Serving: Greyhound
Ingredients:
- 6 cups water, divided
- 2 cups white rice
- 1 cup chopped carrots
- 1 cup baby spinach
- 1 pound ground beef
- 1 cup fresh cranberries

Directions:
1. Place 4 cups of water and the rice in a large saucepan over medium-high heat and bring to a boil. Reduce the heat to low, cover, and simmer until the rice is tender and the water is absorbed for about 20 minutes.
2. Meanwhile, bring the remaining 2 cups of water to a boil in a medium saucepan fitted with a steamer basket. Add the carrots and spinach, cover, and steam for about 10 minutes, or until tender.
3. Heat a large skillet over medium-high heat. Add the beef and sauté until it is cooked through and browned for about 10 minutes.
4. Remove the beef from the heat and drain the excess fat from the skillet. Set aside.
5. Transfer the steamed vegetables to a food processor and purée.
6. Add the vegetables, cooked rice, and cranberries to the beef, stirring to combine.
7. Let cool before serving.
8. Store leftovers in an airtight container or portioned into sealed plastic bags in the refrigerator for up to 1 week or in the freezer for 3 months.

Nutrition: Calories: 459; Fat: 7 g; Fiber: 4 g; Carbs: 32 g; Protein: 32 g

73. Turkey Gravy

Preparation Time: 20 minutes
Cooking Time: 10 minutes
Serving: Beagle
Ingredients:
- 2 cups drippings from the pan
- ¼ cup all-purpose flour
- 1 cup water

Directions:
1. The fat can be filtered out by chilling the drippings and removing the fat from the top. Use ¼ cup of the fat for this recipe.
2. Heat the fat in a large skillet over medium-high heat, then add the flour.
3. Stir continually for about 1 minute. Reduce to the desired thickness by adding turkey drippings, stirring constantly. If needed add some water.
4. Allow cooling fully before using. Use up to one tbsp as a dinner topping. Refrigerate for up to 3 days or freeze for up to 6 months in an airtight container.

Nutrition: Calories: 231.6; Fat: 1.7 g; Net Carbs: 29.8 g; Protein: 25 g

74. Ground Beef and Macaroni

Preparation Time: 10 Minutes
Cooking Time: 30 Minutes
Serving: Shetland Sheepdog
Ingredients:
- 8-ounces dried macaroni
- 2 cups water
- 1 zucchini, chopped
- 1 cup peas
- 1 pound ground beef

Directions:
1. Bring a large pot of water to a boil over high heat. Add the macaroni and cook until al dente, about 8 minutes. Drain the pasta and set aside.
2. Meanwhile, bring the water to a boil in a medium saucepan fitted with a steamer basket. Add the zucchini and peas, cover, and steam for about 10 minutes, or until tender.
3. Heat a large skillet over medium-high heat. Add the beef and sauté until it is cooked through and browned for about 10 minutes.
4. Remove the beef from the heat and drain the excess fat from the skillet.
5. Add the cooked pasta and vegetables to the beef, stirring to combine.
6. Let cool before serving.
7. Store leftovers in an airtight container or portioned into sealed plastic bags in the refrigerator for up to 1 week or in the freezer for 3 months.

Nutrition: Calories: 165; Fat: 5 g; Fiber: 6 g; Carbs: 22 g; Protein: 5 g

75. Cheesy Beef Meal

Preparation Time: 10 Minutes
Cooking Time: 30 Minutes
Serving: Greyhound
Ingredients:
- ¼ pound ground beef
- 2 cups green beans
- 2 cups carrots
- ½ cup cottage cheese

Directions:
1. Brown the beef in a skillet and drain the fat.
2. Allow cooling.
3. Steam the green beans and carrots.
4. Allow cooling.
5. Combine cooled ingredients.
6. Serve a meal and store the remaining.

Nutrition: Calories: 843; Fat: 47 g; Net Carbs: 40 g; Protein: 53 g

76. Wallace Braveheart's Chicken Meatloaf

Preparation Time: 10 minutes

Cooking Time: 1 hour and 45 minutes

Serving: Poodle

Ingredients:

- 1 tbsp olive oil
- ¾ cup carrots, finely chopped
- ½ cup rolled oats
- 2 whole eggs
- ½ cup cottage cheese, low-fat
- 1 ½ pounds ground chicken
- 4 cups homemade chicken broth
- ½ cup barley

Directions:

1. In a pan, bring the chicken broth and barley to a boil, then reduce the heat and simmer for 45 minutes. Set aside to cool.
2. Preheat your oven to 350°F. Lightly spray a baking dish that is 9"x 13" with cooking spray.
3. In a large mixing bowl, mix ground chicken, eggs, rolled oats, cottage cheese, carrots, and olive oil. Mix well to combine. Slowly add the cooled barley to the broth and mix well.
4. Add the mixture to the baking pan and bake for 1 hour.
5. Cool the mixture before serving it to your dog. Store it in the fridge for up to 3 days or freeze it in an airtight container for up to 6 months.

Nutrition: Calories: 236; Fat: 11 g; Net Carbs: 25 g; Protein: 9 g

77. Doggie Meaty

Preparation Time: 10 Minutes

Cooking Time: 30 Minutes

Serving: Poodle

Ingredients:

- 150 g beef for stew
- 30 g sweet potatoes
- 1 tbsp Extra virgin olive oil
- A pinch thyme
- 30 g kefir

Directions:

1. Bring the sweet potato cubes to a boil in a saucepan.
2. In a skillet with olive oil and thyme, lightly sauté the meat.
3. After boiling the sweet potatoes, grate them with the kefir and brewer's yeast.
4. Mash in the meat as well.
5. Allow the cake to rest after combining all of the ingredients.
6. You can finish it in the oven or let it rest at room temperature before serving.

Nutrition: Calories: 276.9; Fat: 9.1 g; Net Carbs: 33 g; Protein: 16.1 g

78. Millet Meal

Preparation Time: 10 Minutes
Cooking Time: 30 Minutes
Serving: Labrador Retriever
Ingredients:
- 1 cup millet
- 2 cups water

Directions:
1. Place a small saucepan over medium heat, add the millet, and toast, stirring occasionally, until it is golden brown, about 5 minutes.
2. Stir in the water and increase the heat to high. Bring the mixture to a boil, then reduce the heat to low, cover, and simmer until tender, about 15 minutes.
3. Remove the saucepan from the heat and let stand for 10 minutes.
4. Fluff the millet with a fork and let it cool.
5. Serve.
6. Store leftovers in an airtight container in the refrigerator for up to 5 days.

Nutrition: Calories: 459; Fat: 7 g; Fiber: 4 g; Carbs: 32 g; Protein: 32 g

79. Mashed Butternut Squash

Preparation Time: 10 Minutes
Cooking Time: 30 Minutes
Serving: Shetland Sheepdog
Ingredients:
- 1 medium butternut squash, peeled, seeded, and chopped
- 2 tbsp olive oil

Directions:
1. Preheat the oven to 400°F. Using parchment paper or aluminum foil, line a baking sheet.
2. Toss the squash and olive oil in a large mixing bowl. Spread the butternut squash on the baking sheet that has been prepared.
3. 30 minutes, or until golden brown, roast the squash.
4. Mash the squash in a large mixing bowl with a potato masher.
5. Before serving, allow the squash to cool.
6. Refrigerate leftovers in an airtight container or portioned into sealed plastic bags for up to 4 days or freeze for 3 months.

Nutrition: Calories: 156; Fat: 3 g; Fiber: 2 g; Carbs: 1 g; Protein: 5 g

80. Chickpea Stew

Preparation Time: 10 Minutes
Cooking Time: 30 Minutes
Serving: Poodle
Ingredients:
- 1 tbsp olive oil
- 1 cup (1⁄4" thick) carrot slices
- 1 tsp peeled and grated fresh ginger
- 2 garlic cloves, minced
- 3 cups cooked chickpeas
- 1½ cups peeled and cubed baking potato
- 1 cup diced green bell pepper
- 1 cup (1) cut green beans
- 1 (14.5-ounce) can diced tomatoes, undrained
- 1¾ cups water or vegetable stock
- 3 cups fresh baby spinach
- 1 cup light coconut milk

Directions:
1. In a large nonstick skillet, heat oil over medium heat. Add carrot and cook until tender, approximately 5 minutes. Stir in ginger and garlic. Cook for 1 minute, stirring constantly to prevent sticking. Remove from heat.
2. Place the mixture in a 5-quart slow cooker. Add chickpeas, potato, bell pepper, green beans, tomatoes, and water or stock. Cook on high for 6 hours or until vegetables are fork-tender.
3. Add spinach and coconut milk, stirring until spinach wilts. Cool before serving to the dog. Refrigerate for up to 3 days.

Nutrition: Calories: 234; Fat: 3 g; Carbs: 21 g; Fiber: 4 g; Protein: 5 g

81. Dehydrated Chicken Liver

Preparation Time: 10 minutes
Cooking Time: 4 hours
Serving: Labrador Retriever
Ingredients:
- 1 pound (450 g) washed chicken liver

Directions:
1. If some of the livers are excessively thick, flatten them slightly with a fork.
2. Place the livers on dehydrator trays, leaving enough space between them to allow for excellent air circulation.
3. Change the position of the drying trays when the livers are noticeably dryer, and let to dehydrate for another 4 hours. Drying times will vary depending on the dehydrator model.
4. Allow the chicken livers to cool completely before storing or serving them.

Nutrition: Calories: 459; Fat: 7 g; Fiber: 4 g; Carbs: 32 g; Protein: 32 g

82. Chicken Jerky

Preparation Time: 10 Minutes
Cooking Time: 30 Minutes
Serving: Poodle
Ingredients:
- 2 to 4 boneless chicken breasts

Directions:
1. Preheat the oven to 200°F.
2. Remove any excess fat from the chicken.
3. Strips should be 18 inches thick.
4. Bake for 2 hours, or until the mixture is dry and hard.
5. Allow cooling completely before serving as a dessert.

Nutrition: Calories: 278; Fat: 10 g; Carbs: 34 g; Protein: 4 g

83. Chicken & Sweet Potato

Preparation Time: 10 Minutes
Cooking Time: 30 Minutes
Serving: Great Dane
Ingredients:
- 2 pounds chicken breast
- ½ cup chopped carrots
- 2 tbsp olive oil
- 1 sweet potato cut into chunks
- 1 cup rice
- ½ cup chopped green beans
- Optional: 1 tbsp rosemary

Directions:
1. Put all the ingredients in a crock pot and simmer on high heat for 5 hours, or until the chicken is cooked thoroughly and everything is mushy.

Nutrition: Calories: 566.7; Fat: 21.2 g; Net Carbs: 72.7 g; Protein: 28.5 g

84. Turmeric Beef

Preparation Time: 10 Minutes
Cooking Time: 30 Minutes
Serving: Golden Retriever
Ingredients:
- 2 pounds beef
- 1 pound broccoli
- 1 cup white rice
- ¼ cup turmeric powder
- 2 tbsp coconut oil

Directions:
1. Thoroughly cook the beef
2. Cook the rice until it is soft.
3. Warm the broccoli.
4. Toss the rice with all of the ingredients.

Nutrition: Calories: 389.4; Fat: 14.8 g; Net Carbs: 40.6 g; Protein: 23.3 g

85. Tuna Balls

Preparation Time: 10 Minutes
Cooking Time: 30 Minutes
Serving: Bulldog
Ingredients:
- 2 pounds canned tuna
- 1 cup rice
- 4 eggs
- ½ pound spinach
- Optional: coconut oil and breadcrumbs

Directions:
1. Cook rice until soft
2. Add eggs and chopped-up spinach to rice and heat until eggs are cooked and spinach has wilted
3. Mix all the ingredients
4. Add a couple of tbsp of coconut oil if the mixture needs to be moister for forming and add a couple of tbsp of breadcrumbs if your puppy's tummy can handle that
5. Either form into balls and refrigerate or keep them as a mixture

Nutrition: Calories: 330; Carbs: 62 g; Fat: 6 g; Protein: 10g

86. Delicious Chicken Meal

Preparation Time: 10 Minutes
Cooking Time: 30 Minutes
Serving: Poodle
Ingredients:
- 2 cups chicken broth or bone broth
- 1 cup cooked chicken
- 1 cup white rice
- 2 cups water

Directions:
1. Combine all ingredients in a large saucepan.
2. Over high heat and bring it to a boil.
3. Reduce to a simmer, cover the pan, and cook until the rice is puffy.
4. Cool completely before serving and refrigerate leftovers.

Nutrition: Calories: 333; Fat: 9.7 g; Net Carbs: 57.1 g; Protein: 5.9 g

87. Spaghetti Squash with Veggies

Preparation Time: 20 minutes
Cooking Time: 40 minutes
Serving: Poodle
Ingredients:

- 1 tsp extra virgin olive oil
- ¼ cup zucchini, diced
- ¼ cup green bell pepper, chopped
- ¼ cup carrots, chopped
- 1 tbsp water
- 1 plum tomato, chopped
- 1 spaghetti squash
- ¼ cup Parmesan cheese, grated

Directions:

1. Preheat the oven to 350°F (180°C).
2. Cut in half lengthwise and scoop out the seeds. Place on a baking tray, flesh side up.
3. Bake for 30–40 minutes or until easily pierced with a fork. Allow cooling before handling.
4. Remove the flesh with a fork and discard the skin. Place cooked squash in a large mixing bowl and set aside.
5. In a large skillet over medium heat, cook the zucchini, bell pepper, and carrots for 5–10 minutes.
6. Cook for a further 5 minutes after adding the tomato and water.
7. Serve over spaghetti squash with cheese on top.
8. Before serving the dog's portion, allow it to cool to room temperature. Refrigerate for up to 5 days or freeze for up to 6 months in an airtight container.

Nutrition: Calories: 291; Fat: 20 g; Net Carbs: 4.4 g; Protein: 24 g

88. Stir Fry Beef Meal

Preparation Time: 10 Minutes
Cooking Time: 30 Minutes
Serving: Beagle
Ingredients:

- 1 pound ground beef, lean
- Small handful whole-wheat pasta
- 1 cup broccoli, chopped
- 4–5 medium-sized, chopped
- 2 cups water

Directions:

1. Bring the beef, carrots, broccoli, and water to a boil in a saucepan.
2. Add the pasta and simmer for about twenty minutes.
3. Allow cooling before serving.

Nutrition: Calories: 244; Fat: 9.1 g; Net Carbs: 28.3 g; Protein: 11.3 g

89. Chicken & Oats

Preparation time: 10 Minutes
Cooking Time: 30 Minutes
Serving: Poodle
Ingredients:

- ½ cup chopped parsley
- 2 pounds chicken breast
- 1 cup rice
- ⅔ cups quick cooking oats
- 2 cups spinach
- ½ cup plain yogurt
- 2 tablespoons olive oil
- ½ cup carrots

Directions:

1. Cook rice until tender.
2. Chop the spinach and carrots after being steamed until soft
3. Completely cook the chicken after draining the water
4. Add all ingredients together

Nutrition: Calories 252.8, Fat: 8g, Net Carbs: 19.8g, Protein: 25.6g

90. Sweet Potatoes Meal

Preparation time: 10 Minutes
Cooking Time: 30 Minutes
Serving: Shetland Sheepdog
Ingredients:

- 2 sweet potatoes, scrubbed and halved lengthwise

Directions:

1. Preheat the oven to 400°F. Line a baking sheet with parchment paper or aluminum foil.
2. Place the sweet potatoes, cut-side up, on the baking sheet. Bake until tender, 25 to 35 minutes.
3. Cool the potatoes, then cut them into bite-size chunks.
4. Serve.
5. Store leftovers in an airtight container in the refrigerator for up to 3 days.

Nutrition: calories 125, fat 5g, fiber 4g, carbs 12g, protein 5g

91. Strips of Dried Beef

Preparation time: 15 minutes
Cooking time: 3 hours
Serving: Shetland Sheepdog
Ingredients:

- Skirt steak, 1 lb. (450g)

Directions:

1. Preheat the oven to 300°F (150°C) or use a food dehumidifier. Prepare a baking sheet.
2. Cut the beef into 12-inch-wide strips. (1.2 cm). Place the sheets on the baking sheet, but make sure they are not touching.
3. Reduce the oven temperature to 200°F (95°C) after 1 hour of baking. Allow moisture to escape by slightly opening the oven door. Bake the strips for an additional 2 hours.
4. Take the strips out of the oven and place them on a wire drying rack to cool completely.

Nutrition: calories 125, fat 5g, fiber 4g, carbs 12g, protein 5g

92. Chicken Gravy

Preparation time: 10 minutes
Cooking time: 10 minutes
Serving: Poodle
Ingredients:

- 2 tbsp melted butter
- 2 tbsp flour (all-purpose)
- Homemade Chicken Broth (1 ¼ Cups)
- ½ gallon (1.8l) milk

Directions:

1. Melt the butter in a large skillet over medium heat. Cook for 1 minute in the butter, stirring constantly, after whisking in the flour.
2. Stir in the broth and milk for about 2 minutes to thicken. Take the pan off the heat and set it aside to cool.
3. As a meal topping, use up to 1 tbsp. In an airtight container, store for up to 3 days or freeze for up to 6 months.

Nutrition: Calories 222.8, Fat: 0.9g, Net Carbs: 21.7g, Protein: 25.4g

93. Eggshell Dog Meal

Preparation time: 30 minutes
Cooking time: 15 minutes
Serving: Bulldog
Ingredients:
- 12 eggshells or more

Directions:

1. Refrigerate washed eggshells until you have enough to cover a baking tray.
2. Preheat the oven to 200°F (95°C).
3. Bake the eggshells for 10–15 minutes after spreading them out on a baking tray. Allow extra baking time if you scrubbed the eggshells right before baking. Before grinding, the eggshells must be completely dry.
4. With a mortar and pestle, grind to a fine powder. You can also use a clean coffee grinder or blender. If using a blender, make sure to grind the eggshells until all large pieces are ground to a powder.
5. Store in a jar with a cover. Store for up to 2 months in a dry location.

Nutrition: Calories 300, Fat: 15g, Net Carbs: 6g, Protein: 31g

Side Dishes

94. Cheesy Eggs and Rice

Preparation Time: 10 Minutes
Cooking Time: 30 Minutes
Serving: Golden Retriever
Ingredients:
- 6 scrambled eggs
- ½ cup cottage cheese
- 1 cup cooked brown rice

Directions:
1. Mix ingredients and cook together.

Nutrition: Calories: 343; Fat: 14 g; Carbs: 55 g; Fiber: 8 g; Protein: 6 g

95. Vegetable Fish Patties

Preparation Time: 10 Minutes
Cooking Time: 30 Minutes
Serving: Bulldog
Ingredients:
- 2 cans salmon
- 2 potatoes
- 2 carrots
- 2 cooked eggs
- 2 celery stalks
- 5 tbsp flour

Directions:
1. Drain the salmon and fry it with the flour and eggs.
2. Take the patties out of the oil.
3. For five to eight minutes, stir the vegetables in the oil.
4. Set aside to cool after mixing everything.
5. As desired, serve or store.

Nutrition: Calories: 244; Fat: 6 g; Carbs: 30 g; Fiber: 6 g; Protein: 7 g

96. Green Eggs & Beef

Preparation Time: 10 Minutes
Cooking Time: 30 Minutes
Serving: Bulldog
Ingredients:
- 2 pounds beef
- 5 eggs
- 1 bunch kale
- 1 cup broth
- ¼ cup kelp powder

Directions:
1. Cook beef properly and drain any grease.
2. Simmer the kale and kelp in the broth until it is warm, about 5 minutes.
3. Heat the stock with the eggs and meat until the eggs are cooked.
4. Allow cooling before serving.

Nutrition: Calories: 275; Fat: 10 g; Carbs: 38 g; Protein: 4g

97. Italian Spinach Balls

Preparation Time: 10 Minutes
Cooking Time: 30 Minutes
Serving: Beagle
Ingredients:

- 1 cup frozen chopped spinach
- 1 tbsp olive oil
- ¾ cup whole wheat flour
- ¾ cup rolled oats
- 2 tbsp grated Parmesan cheese, reduced fat
- 1 tsp dried oregano

Directions:

1. Preheat the oven to 350°F.
2. Do not squeeze the spinach to remove any additional moisture.
3. Combine the chopped spinach and olive oil in a small dish.
4. In a large mixing bowl, combine the flour, oats, cheese, and oregano.
5. Make a well in the center of the flour mixture to add the spinach.
6. Stir until thoroughly combined.
7. Begin kneading the dough in the basin. If necessary, add 2 tbsp of water to help the dough come together.
8. Lightly spray a baking sheet with nonstick cooking spray.
9. Using a 1-inch cookie scooper, make spherical balls and arrange them on a baking sheet.
10. Bake for 30 minutes in the oven.
11. Allow cooling on a wire rack.

Nutrition: Calories: 224.9; Fat: 4.8 g; Net Carbs: 29.2 g; Protein: 16.5 g

98. Bites of Anchovy

Preparation Time: 10 minutes
Cooking Time: 25 minutes
Serving: Dachshund
Ingredients:

- 1 can (2 ounces/50 g) anchovies in olive oil (do not drain)
- 1 cup water
- 1 egg
- ½ cup oats, rolled
- ½ cup flour (whole wheat)
- 4 tsp parsley, finely chopped (fresh or dry)

Directions:

1. Preheat the oven to 350°F (180°C). Line a baking tray with parchment paper or grease it.
2. In a blender, purée the anchovies, water, and egg.
3. In a big mixing basin, combine the oats, flour, and parsley. Fully incorporate the anchovy paste.
4. Make little dough balls with a small scoop and place them on a baking tray.
5. Bake for 25 minutes until golden brown.
6. Allow cooling completely before serving or storing.

Nutrition: Calories: 233; Fat: 13 g; Net Carbs: 11 g; Protein: 26g

99. Hearty Potato

Preparation Time: 10 Minutes
Cooking Time: 30 Minutes
Serving: Chihuahua
Ingredients:

- 150g beef or lamb heart
- 100g white potato
- ½ cup oatmeal
- ½ zucchini
- 2 carrots
- A pinch turmeric and rosemary
- 2 tbsp Sunflower or corn oil

Directions:

1. Chop and peel the ingredients into smaller cubes appropriate for your dog's size.
2. Boil the potatoes, zucchini, and carrots.
3. Cook the meat lightly on the grill or in a preheated oven, using vegetable oil.
4. Add the spices to flavor the heart as well.
5. Wait until the potatoes and vegetables are done.
6. Combine all of the ingredients, including the oatmeal, and mash the potatoes with a fork.
7. Allow cooling before serving.

Nutrition: Calories: 47; Fat: 0.3 g; Net Carbs: 0.7 g; Protein: 0.7g

100. Vegetable side dish

Preparation Time: 10 Minutes
Cooking Time: 30 Minutes
Serving: Beagle
Ingredients:

- 1 breast lean chicken
- 1 cup mixed vegetables (broccoli, sweet potato, carrot, zucchini)
- 2 cups Brown rice (optional)

Directions:

1. Set the oven to 350°F.
2. Cook the chicken breast (do not add any salt or seasoning). Slices of vegetables should be steam-cooked while retaining some crunch.
3. Slice the cooked chicken into bite-sized pieces, mix it with the vegetables (but make sure there is more meat than vegetables), and give your dog the suggested serving size. Save the rest for another day.

Nutrition: Calories: 250; Fat: 3 g; Net Carbs: 37 g; Protein: 14g

101. Pumpkin Cookies

Preparation Time: 10 Minutes
Cooking Time: 30 Minutes
Serving: Dachshund
Ingredients:

- 1 cup pumpkin purée
- 2 large eggs
- 3 cups whole-wheat flour, divided, plus more for flouring

Directions:

1. Preheat the oven to 350°F. Set aside a baking sheet lined with parchment paper or a silicone baking mat.
2. For 1 to 2 minutes on medium-high speed, beat the pumpkin and eggs in the bowl of an electric mixer fitted with the paddle attachment.
3. Reduce the speed to low and gradually add 2 1/2 cups of flour, mixing only until combined.
4. ¼ cups at a time, beat in the remaining flour until the dough is no longer sticky.
5. Knead the dough a few times on a lightly floured surface until it comes together.
6. Roll the dough out to a 14-inch thickness with a rolling pin.
7. Cut out the desired shapes with cookie cutters and place them on the prepared baking sheet.
8. Bake the cookies for 20 to 25 minutes, or until the edges are golden brown.
9. Allow the cookies to cool completely after removing them from the oven.
10. Store the cookies in an airtight container at room temperature for up to 3 days or in the freezer for up to 3 months.

Nutrition: Calories: 165; Fat: 5 g; Fiber: 6 g; Carbs: 22 g; Protein: 5 g

102. Fish and Peanut Cookies

Preparation Time: 10 Minutes
Cooking Time: 30 Minutes
Serving: Greyhound
Ingredients:

- 2 cups flour
- 1 cup Rolled oats
- ½ cup smooth peanut butter
- 1 tbsp Honey
- ½ tsp fish oil
- 1 ¾ cups Water

Directions:

1. Set the oven to 350°F.
2. In a sizable bowl, combine the flour and the oats.
3. Add a cup of water, then blend until smooth.
4. Add fish oil, honey, and peanut butter. Combine once more.
5. While continuing to mix, slowly add ¼ cup of water.
6. Cut To be shaped. Bake For 40 minutes.
7. Cool, then dish.

Nutrition: Calories: 370; Fat: 17 g; Net Carbs: 14 g; Protein: 38 g

103. Dried Beet Chips

Preparation Time: 10 Minutes
Cooking Time: 30 Minutes
Serving: Poodle
Ingredients:

- 1 can sliced beets

Directions:

1. Set the oven to 350°F.
2. Use parchment paper to cover a baking sheet.
3. Beets should be drained and rinsed until the water is clear.
4. Slices of beet should be arranged in one layer.
5. For 35 minutes, bake. Allow them to rest for ten minutes after turning off the oven.
6. Cool on a wire rack.

Nutrition: Calories: 287; Fat: 26.3 g; Net Carbs: 15 g; Protein: 26.3 g

104. Fruit Parfait

Preparation Time: 10 Minutes
Cooking Time: 30 Minutes
Serving: Beagle
Ingredients:
- ½ cup plain yogurt
- ½ cup strawberries (diced)
- ½ cup blueberries(chopped)
- ½ cup Applesauce

Directions:
1. In a bowl, combine the ingredients. Blend, then serve.

Nutrition: Calories: 235.4; Fat: 11.9 g; Net Carbs: 6.9 g; Protein: 24 g

105. Healthy Homemade Strips for Dogs

Preparation Time: 10 Minutes
Cooking Time: 30 Minutes
Serving: Rottweiler
Ingredients:
- 1 little sweet potato
- 1 large banana
- 1 cup minced carrots
- ½ cup unsweetened applesauce
- 1 cup wheat flour
- 1 cup Rolled oats
- ¼ cup water

Directions:
1. Set the oven to 350°F.
2. For 9 minutes, microwave sweet potatoes.
3. In a big bowl, mash the sweet potato and banana.
4. Add oats, flour, and carrots. Mix well.
5. Applesauce and water should be combined carefully.
6. Cut the rolled-out dough into strips.
7. Bake for 25 minutes.

Nutrition: Calories: 470; Fat: 13 g; Net Carbs: 63 g; Protein: 27g

106. Bacon Bites

Preparation Time: 10 Minutes
Cooking Time: 30 Minutes
Serving: Shetland Sheepdog
Ingredients:
- 1 sweet potato, peeled and cut into 1-inch chunks
- 2 bacon slices, cooked
- 2 large eggs
- 3 cups almond flour, plus more for flouring

Directions:
1. Preheat the oven to 350°F. Set aside a large baking sheet lined with parchment paper or aluminum foil.
2. In a medium saucepan over high heat, place the sweet potato. 1 inch of water should be added to cover the sweet potato. Bring to a boil, then reduce to low heat, cover, and cook for 30 minutes, or until the sweet potato is tender.
3. Drain and place the sweet potato in a food processor. Purée the mixture with the bacon.
4. Fill the bowl of an electric mixer fitted with the paddle attachment halfway with the sweet potato and bacon mixture. Add the eggs and mix on medium speed until combined.
5. Mix in the almond flour until a tacky dough forms. If the dough is too sticky, add 1 tbsp of flour at a time (but no more than 12 cup total).
6. Knead the dough a few times on a lightly floured surface until it comes together.
7. Roll out the dough to a 14-inch thickness with a lightly floured rolling pin.
8. Cut out the desired shapes with cookie cutters and place them on the prepared baking sheet.
9. Bake the treats for about 20 minutes, or until they are dry and the edges are golden. Flip the treats with tongs or a spatula and bake for another 10 minutes.
10. Allow the treats to cool completely after removing them from the oven.
11. Store the treats in an airtight container at room temperature for up to 3 days or in the freezer for up to 3 months.

Nutrition: Calories: 120; Carbs: 62 g; Fat: 6 g; Protein: 10g

107. Kiwi and Canine Kale

Preparation Time: 5 minutes
Cooking Time: 10 minutes
Serving: German Shepherd
Ingredients:
- 1 tbsp coconut oil
- 1 tsp fresh ginger, peeled and minced
- 1 tbsp oregano leaves, fresh
- 2 peeled and sliced kiwis
- 1 bunch kale, washed and thinly sliced

Directions:
1. Thinly slice the kale leaves. Peel and slice the Kiwi, then finely mince the ginger.
2. In a large skillet, cook the ginger in coconut oil for three minutes over medium-high heat. After that, add the oregano and kiwi and continue stirring for another 2 minutes.
3. Reduce the heat to low and add the kale; simmer for at least 5 minutes until soft.
4. Allow cooling before serving. Refrigerate for up to 3 days.

Nutrition: Calories: 459; Fat: 30 g; Carbs: 52 g; Fiber: 19 g; Protein: 8 g

108. Easter Carrot Cookies

Preparation Time: 30 minutes
Cooking Time: 30 minutes
Serving: Chihuahua
Ingredients:
- 2 cups oats, rolled
- 2 cups flour (all-purpose)
- 1 cup carrots, grated
- 2 tbsp molasses
- 2 large eggs
- ½ cup butter
- 2 tbsp powdered baking soda
- ½ cup water

Frosting:
- 4-ounces (110g) cream cheese

Directions:
1. Preheat the oven to 350°F (180°C). Prepare two baking trays with parchment paper.
2. Combine all of the ingredients (except for the cream cheese) in a large mixing basin and mix well until everything is thoroughly combined.
3. On a lightly floured surface, roll out the dough to a thickness of ¼ inches (0,5cm). Cut out the dough into cookie shapes.
4. Bake for 30 minutes or until golden brown. Allow the cookies to cool completely before sandwiching them with softened cream cheese between two cookies.
5. Refrigerate for up to 5 Scottie's Scotch Eggs

Nutrition: Calories: 35; Fat: 1 g; Net Carbs: 6 g; Protein: 1 g

109. Sweet Potato Potstickers

Preparation Time: 30 minutes
Cooking Time: 20 minutes
Serving: Greyhound
Ingredients:
- 1 cup sweet potato, cooked (roughly 2 medium sweet potatoes, peeled)
- 1 tbsp fresh rosemary
- ⅓ cup ricotta cheese
- 1 pack wonton wrappers
- ¼ cup grated Parmesan cheese
- 1 tsp sunflower seed oil

Directions:
1. Preheat the oven to 350°F (180°C).
2. Combine the sweet potato, rosemary, and cheese in a blender or food processor. Pulse until everything is well combined.
3. Place 1 tbsp of the sweet potato and cheese stuffing in the center of a wonton wrapper; seal the edges with oil to keep them closed. Arrange the wontons on a baking sheet.
4. To coat the wontons, use sunflower oil.
5. Bake for 15–20 minutes, or until the top is golden brown.
6. Allow cooling before serving or refrigerating your dog. Refrigerate for 3 days or freeze in an airtight container for up to 6 months.

Nutrition: Calories: 459; Fat: 30 g; Carbs: 52 g; Fiber: 19 g; Protein: 8 g

110. Cheerios and Peanut Butter Balls

Preparation Time: 10 Minutes
Cooking Time: 30 Minutes
Serving: Shetland Sheepdog
Ingredients:
- ½ cup peanut butter (chunky)
- 2 eggs
- 1 ½ cups Cheerios (Honey Nut)
- 5 tbsp vegetable oil
- ¾ cup all-purpose flour

Directions:
1. Set up the oven at 350°F and warm the peanut butter in the microwave for about a minute.
2. Add all the ingredients to a large bowl, and mix gently until the mixture forms a sticky consistency.
3. Use a tbsp to drop the mixture on a paper-lined baking tray.
4. Bake the treats until they are golden brown.

Nutrition: Calories: 120; Carbs: 62 g; Fat: 6 g; Protein: 10g

111. Hot Chili

Preparation Time: 10 Minutes
Cooking Time: 30 Minutes
Serving: Shetland Sheepdog
Ingredients:
- 4 chicken breasts, sliced
- 4 cups chicken stock
- 1 cup black beans, drained
- 1 cup kidney beans, drained
- 1 cup carrots, chopped
- ½ tomato paste

Directions:
1. Chicken should be cooked through in a skillet over medium-high heat.
2. Cooked chicken, beans, carrots, tomato paste, and chicken broth should all be added to the saucepan.
3. For ten minutes, cook over medium heat.
4. Cool, then dish.

Nutrition: Calories: 150; Fat: 5 g; Net Carbs: 15 g; Protein: 11 g

112. Casserole Slices

Preparation Time: 10 Minutes
Cooking Time: 30 Minutes
Serving: Chihuahua
Ingredients:
- 2 chicken breasts (chopped)
- 2 cups chicken stock
- 1 cup veggies, chopped (variety mix—your choice)
- ¼ cup rolled oats
- 2 tbsp Vegetable oil

Directions:
1. Cook chicken in a frying pan with oil.
2. Fill the pan with the chopped vegetables, chicken broth, and rolled oats.
3. Cook for ten minutes.

Nutrition: Calories: 100; Fat: 3.7 g; Net Carbs: 0 g; Protein: 16 g

113. Crunchy Snacks

Preparation Time: 10 Minutes
Cooking Time: 30 Minutes
Serving: Shetland Sheepdog
Ingredients:
- 6 cups white, whole wheat, or oat flour
- 4 medium eggs or 3 big eggs
- 1 cup milk powder
- 30 ml baking oil
- 2 basins for mixing
- 2 ½ cups water, milk, or broth2 wooden spoons

Directions:
1. Preheat your oven to 350°F. Before storing a cookie sheet, lightly spray it with baking spray.
2. Combine flour and milk powder in a mixing bowl. Set the bowl aside after giving the ingredients one last stir with a wooden spoon.
3. In the second mixing dish, thoroughly combine the eggs, baking oil, and liquid of choice with a wooden spoon.
4. Combine the dry and wet ingredients to make a thick, moist dough that resembles bread. Add any additional ingredients you want to include, such as cheese, shredded meat, pureed fruits, or vegetables. If the dough is too dry, add more liquid, and if it is too moist, add more flour.
5. Spread the kibble dough onto the oiled cookie sheet with a wooden spoon until it is about half an inch thick. Place the tray in the oven.
6. After 45 minutes of baking, they should be golden brown and firm to the touch. The baking sheet should be removed from the oven and set aside to cool.
7. Remove the baked "cookie" from the baking sheet and cut it into bite-sized pieces for your dog. Refrigerate the crunchy dog food in an airtight container.

Nutrition: Calories: 110.8; Fat: 6.3 g; Net Carbs: 9.2 g; Protein: 6.8 g

114. Potato Chicken Side Dish

Preparation Time: 10 Minutes
Cooking Time: 30 Minutes
Serving: Labrador Retriever
Ingredients:
- ½ cup cooked chicken
- 6 cups boiled potatoes
- 4 tbsp chicken fat
- 3 calcium carbonate tablets
- 1 multiple vitamin-mineral tablets

Directions:
1. Cook all the ingredients together.
2. Add tablets last when the meat is almost ready.
3. Stir and serve or store as desired.

Nutrition: Calories: 343; Fat: 14 g; Carbs: 55 g; Fiber: 8 g; Protein: 6 g

115. Sage Chicken & Sweet Potato

Preparation Time: 10 Minutes
Cooking Time: 30 Minutes
Serving: Beagle
Ingredients:
- 2 pounds chicken
- 2 sweet potatoes
- 4 tbsp olive oil
- ½ pound spinach
- About 15 sage leaves (or half a package)

Directions:
1. Cook the chicken until cooked thoroughly.
2. Pierce sweet potato with a fork and microwave for 8 minutes.
3. Heat olive oil in a pan on the stove, insert the sage leaves and cook on medium heat for 3 minutes.
4. Add spinach leaves and cook until wilted.
5. Chop the cooked spinach and add all ingredients together, and serve.

Nutrition: Calories: 204; Fat: 1.4 g; Net Carbs: 24.1 g; Protein: 23.9 g

116. Salmon Medley

Preparation Time: 10 Minutes
Cooking Time: 30 Minutes
Serving: Golden Retriever
Ingredients:
- 2 pounds salmon
- 1 cup peas
- 1 cup rice
- ½ cup cauliflower

Directions:
1. Bake salmon (except using canned).
2. Cook rice until soft.
3. Steam the veggies.
4. Mix everything and serve.

Nutrition: Calories: 376.7; Fat: 9.8 g; Net Carbs: 49.4 g; Protein: 27 g

117. Chicken, Apple, Leafy Medley

Preparation Time: 10 Minutes
Cooking Time: 30 Minutes
Serving: Chihuahua
Ingredients:
- 5 eggs
- 4 pounds chicken breast
- 2 skinned apples
- 4 cups spinach
- 2 tbsp olive oil

Directions:
1. Boil chicken in stock pot until fully done.
2. Place all other ingredients in the pot, except eggs, and simmer for 10 minutes.
3. Turn off the oven and add the eggs.
4. Stir everything up, allow to cool, and serve and store leftovers!

Nutrition: Calories: 77; Fat: 3.4 g; Net Carbs: 2.5 g; Protein: 9.3 g

118. Carrot Cookies

Preparation Time: 10 Minutes
Cooking Time: 30 Minutes
Serving: Shetland Sheepdog
Ingredients:

- ½ cup coconut oil (virgin)
- 2 cups whole wheat flour
- 2 cups carrots (shredded)
- 1 egg
- ¾ cup water
- 1 pinch cinnamon powder

Directions:

1. Preheat the oven to 330°F. Using parchment paper, line a baking sheet.
2. In a large mixing bowl, combine all of the wet ingredients. Stir in the carrots once the mixture has been thoroughly blended. After that, gently fold in the flour and cinnamon powder until the mixture reaches a doughy consistency.
3. Roll out the dough to a thickness of 1/4 inch on a flat surface. Using your preferred cookie cutter, cut out cookie shapes.
4. Arrange the cookies on the baking sheet and bake for 30 minutes. After baking, leave the cookies in the oven for 15 minutes.
5. When completely cool, serve

Nutrition: Calories: 120; Carbs: 62 g; Fat: 6 g; Protein: 10 g

119. Simple Crispy Cheese

Preparation Time: 5 minutes
Cooking Time: 5 minutes
Serving: Shetland Sheepdog
Ingredients:

- 1 cup shredded hard cheese, such as Asiago, Parmesan, or Romano
- 1 tsp powdered cinnamon or ginger (optional)

Directions:

1. Preheat the oven to 350°F (180°C). Line two baking trays with parchment paper.
2. Mix the spice powder with the cheese if using.
3. Simply layer or stack about 1 tbsp of cheese onto the baking trays. Allow some space between the treats because they will spread out. Even out the piles so that each one is about the same height.
1. Bake for 5 minutes.
4. Allow cooling before serving. Keep refrigerated for up to 5 days.

Nutrition: Calories: 125; Fat: 5 g; Fiber: 4 g; Carbs: 12 g; Protein: 5 g

120. Kale Chips

Preparation Time: 10 Minutes
Cooking Time: 30 Minutes
Serving: Great Dane
Ingredients:

- 1 head kale, washed and dried
- 2 tbsp olive oil

Directions:

1. Preheat oven to 275°F.
2. Remove ribs from the kale and trim to 2" pieces. In a plastic bag, toss pieces with olive oil. Remove from the bag and spread pieces on a cookie sheet.
3. Bake kale until crisp (about 20 minutes), turning leaves halfway.

Nutrition: Calories: 844.4; Fat: 82.3 g; Net Carbs: 7 g; Protein: 22.2 g

121. Chicken Risotto

Preparation Time: 10 Minutes
Cooking Time: 30 Minutes
Serving: Shetland Sheepdog
Ingredients:
- 150g chicken or turkey meat
- 30g white rice
- 2 eggs
- ½ yogurt
- 20g asparagus
- 2 tbsp Corn oil
- 2 tbsp Chicken risotto

Directions:
1. Bring two eggs to a boil in a pot and remove when fully cooked.
2. Using a grater, grate the boiled eggs.
3. In a separate bowl, crush the egg shells.
4. Chicken should be cut into small cubes.
5. Bring a pot of water to a boil in another.
6. Sauté the asparagus in a pot with the rice and some boiling water.
7. To avoid sticking, constantly stir the asparagus and rice.
8. Every time the rice absorbs water, add more. When it's almost done, add the chicken pieces and the grated egg.
9. Don't forget to add half of the yogurt and the crushed egg shells at the end.

Nutrition: Calories: 140; Fat: 7 g; Fiber: 6 g; Carbs: 22 g; Protein: 7 g

122. Kale Nachos

Preparation Time: 10 Minutes
Cooking Time: 30 Minutes
Serving: Golden Retriever
Ingredients:
- 2 bunches Kale
- 1 can black beans (no salt added)
- 1 pound ground beef
- 2 tbsp olive oil

Directions:
1. Cook ground beef until cooked through, and drain excess fat.
2. Add black beans to ground beef.
3. Heat a separate pan over medium heat and add 2 tbsp of olive oil.
4. Separate kale leaves from the stem and put them in the pan.
5. Heat kale for about 10 minutes on the pan or until they are crisp.
6. Mix kale ground beef and beans, and serve.

Nutrition: Calories: 375; Fat: 13 g; Net Carbs: 26 g; Protein: 35g

123. Deli Turkey Rollups

Preparation Time: 10 Minutes
Cooking Time: 30 Minutes
Serving: Shetland Sheepdog
Ingredients:
- 2-ounces cream cheese
- ¼ pound sliced low-sodium turkey breast

Directions:
1. Spread 1–2 tbsp of cream cheese on a slice of turkey breast.
2. Roll up tightly, then slice into 1" pieces.
3. Refrigerate for up to 3 days, storing flat to keep the treats from unrolling.

Nutrition: Calories: 112; Fat: 6.2 g; Net Carbs: 7.1 g; Protein: 7 g

Treats

124. Caribbean Canine Coolers

Preparation Time: 10 Minutes
Cooking Time: 30 Minutes
Serving: Chihuahua
Ingredients:
- 3 cups yogurt (plain)
- 1 cup unsweetened crushed coconut flakes
- 1 tbsp molasses (blackstrap)
- 2 peeled huge mango
- 2 peeled bananas

Directions:
1. In a blender, combine all of the components and mix for 1–2 minutes until smooth.
2. Freeze this mixture in ice cube trays or tiny plastic tubs half-filled with it for delicious island treats for you and your dog!

Nutrition: Calories: 100; Fat: 2.5 g; Net Carbs: 1 g; Protein: 6 g

125. Frozen Fruit Popsicles

Preparation Time: 10 Minutes
Cooking Time: 30 Minutes
Serving: Poodle
Ingredients:
- 1 cup fresh fruit choice, cored and diced (no grapes or raisins!)
- 4 cups water
- 1 tbsp molasses (blackstrap) (optional)

Directions:
1. In a large mixing bowl, combine the fruit, water, and molasses (if using).
2. Place the mixture in small tubs or ice cube trays to freeze. Once frozen, store in a zip-top plastic bag in the freezer for up to 6 months.

Nutrition: Calories: 280; Fat: 7.1 g; Net Carbs: 30 g; Protein: 23.9 g

126. Watermelon Slush

Preparation Time: 10 Minutes
Cooking Time: 30 Minutes
Serving: Poodle
Ingredients:
- 2 cups cubed seedless watermelon
- ½ cup strawberries, hulled
- 1 tbsp molasses
- ½ cup coconut water
- 1 cup ice

Directions:
1. Combine all ingredients in a blender and mix.
2. Serve in a bowl as a slushy treat, or pour into a KONG® and freeze for long-lasting cooling fun.
3. Share a Slice of Fun

Nutrition: Calories: 276.9; Fat: 11.4 g; Net Carbs: 18.6 g; Protein: 26.1 g

127. Pumpkin Ice Cream

Preparation Time: 10 Minutes
Cooking Time: 30 Minutes
Serving: Poodle
Ingredients:
- 1 cup Pumpkin Purée
- 1 cup low-fat plain yogurt
- ½ cup organic unsweetened peanut butter

Directions:
1. Combine all ingredients in a blender, then pour into ice cube trays.
2. Freeze and serve frozen. Freeze in an airtight container for up to 6 months.

Nutrition: Calories: 287; Fat: 12 g; Carbs: 41 g; Fiber: 6 g; Protein: 8 g

128. Cream Cheese Icing

Preparation Time: 10 Minutes
Cooking Time: 30 Minutes
Serving: Bulldog
Ingredients:

- 8-ounces (225g) cream cheese
- 2 tbsp plain low-fat yogurt
- 2–3 tbsp flour (all-purpose)

Directions:

1. In a mixing bowl, combine cream cheese and yogurt. Add the flour in a thin stream, mixing well after each addition until you reach the desired consistency.
2. After decorating, keep the frosting and treats refrigerated. Refrigerate for up to 5 days or freeze for up to 6 months in an airtight container.

Nutrition: Calories: 316; Fat: 28 g; Net Carbs: 3.9 g; Protein: 23.9 g

129. Cheese Training Treats

Preparation Time: 30 minutes
Cooking Time: 15 minutes
Serving: Chihuahua
Ingredients:

- 1 cup flour (whole wheat)
- 1 cup Cheddar cheese, grated
- 1 tbsp soy sauce
- 1 tbsp softened butter
- ½ gallon (1,9l) milk

Directions:

1. Preheat the oven to 350°F (180°C) or use a food dehumidifier. Line or grease a baking sheet with parchment paper.
2. In a large mixing bowl, combine all ingredients except the milk by hand. Incorporate the milk a little at a time until all of the ingredients are combined.
3. Knead the dough on a floured surface and roll it out to a 14-inch thickness. (6mm).
4. Cut dough into desired cookie shapes and place on baking sheet. Bake for 15 minutes, or until the top is golden brown.
5. Turn off the oven, slightly crack the oven door, and allow the goodies to cool completely in the oven to make them extremely crispy.
6. Store in an airtight container for up to 5 days or freeze for up to 6 months.

Nutrition: Calories: 62.38; Fat: 1.6 g; Net Carbs: 12.3 g; Protein: 1.9 g

130. Pumpkin Peanut Butter Homemade Dog Treats

Preparation Time: 10 Minutes
Cooking Time: 30 Minutes
Serving: Poodle
Ingredients:
- 1 ¾ cups whole grain brown rice flour
- 1 cup 100% pure pumpkin puree, canned
- ½ cup natural peanut butter

Directions:
1. Preheat oven to 350°F and line cookie sheet with parchment paper.
2. Stir the peanut butter and pumpkin together in a large bowl.
3. Stir in the flour ¼ cup at a time, just until the dough is no longer sticky.
4. Roll the dough out between two sheets of parchment paper to ¼ inch thick.
5. Use a cookie cutter to cut out the dough and place it on a cookie sheet.
6. Bake at 350°F for 8 to 10 minutes, let cool, and store in an airtight container.

Nutrition: Calories: 248.2; Fat: 4 g; Net Carbs: 22.9 g; Protein: 27.7 g

131. Mashed Potato Icing

Preparation Time: 15 minutes
Cooking Time: 25 minutes
Serving: Chihuahua
Ingredients:
- 10 potatoes, a medium size
- 2 tbsp fresh parsley chopped
- 2 quarts (2 l) water
- 2 tbsp sour cream

Directions:
1. Peel and wash potatoes, removing any green spots. Cubed potatoes should be placed in a large saucepan. Add the parsley and cover with water.
2. Bring to a boil, then reduce to low heat for 25 minutes.
3. Drain the potatoes and parsley and mash them with a fork or a potato masher.
4. Combine with sour cream. To make a smooth, lump-free mixture, use a fork or a whisk.
5. Remove from the oven and set aside to cool completely before serving. In an airtight container, store for up to 5 days or freeze for up to 6 months.

Nutrition: Calories: 27; Fat: 0.3 g; Net Carbs: 5.1 g; Protein: 0.8g

132. Sorbet de Mango

Preparation Time: 10 Minutes
Cooking Time: 30 Minutes
Serving: Beagle
Ingredients:
- 2 peeled ripe mangos
- 1 orange juice
- ½ cup almond milk, unsweetened

Directions:
1. Purée all of the ingredients in a blender.
2. Fill an ice cube tray halfway with the mixture.
3. Freeze for at least 24 hours. Transfer frozen cubes to a zip-top plastic bag and keep them in the freezer for up to 2 months.

Nutrition: Calories: 245; Fat: 9 g; Net Carbs: 8 g; Protein: 31 g

133. Peanut Butter and Banana Dog Ice Cream

Preparation Time: 10 Minutes
Cooking Time: 30 Minutes
Serving: Shetland Sheepdog
Ingredients:
- 3–4 ripe bananas
- 4 cups low-fat plain yogurt
- ½ cup organic unsweetened peanut butter

Directions:
1. Peel bananas and add to a blender along with yogurt and peanut butter.
2. Blend until smooth, then pour into ice cube trays.
3. Freeze and serve frozen. Freeze in an airtight container for up to 6 months.

Nutrition: Calories: 102.6; Fat: 1.5 g; Net Carbs: 3.6 g; Protein: 18 g

134. Pumpkin Treats

Preparation Time: 10 Minutes
Cooking Time: 30 Minutes
Serving: Greyhound
Ingredients:
- 2 cups coconut flour
- ½ cup all-natural peanut butter
- 1 cup pure pumpkin
- 2 eggs

Directions:
1. Heat the oven to 350°F.
2. Blend or whisk ingredients together.
3. Place into the desired pan.
4. Bake for 10 to 15 minutes.

Nutrition: Calories: 468; Fat: 26 g; Net Carbs: 17 g; Protein: 38 g

135. Cheesy Biscuits

Preparation Time: 10 Minutes
Cooking Time: 30 Minutes
Serving: Bulldog
Ingredients:
- 2.5 cups whole wheat flour or oats
- ½ cup beef or chicken stock
- 1 egg
- ½ cup cream cheese
- ½ cup bacon bits

Directions:
1. Mix into a dough.
2. Cut into biscuits.
3. Bake for 30 minutes.

Nutrition: Calories: 265.2; Fat: 7.6 g; Net Carbs: 12.2 g; Protein: 35.2 g

136. Blueberry Fruit Rollups

Preparation Time: 10 Minutes
Cooking Time: 30 Minutes
Serving: Shetland Sheepdog
Ingredients:
- 1 pound fresh or frozen blueberries
- 1 tbsp lemon juice
- 1 tbsp raw honey

Directions:
1. Preheat the oven to 170°F. Use parchment paper to line a cookie sheet.
2. Blend all of the ingredients in a blender until smooth. If necessary, add a tbsp of water.
3. Spread the mixture on parchment paper, avoiding the paper's edges.
4. Bake the rollups for 6–7 hours, or until they are no longer sticky. Remove from the oven and allow to cool completely.
5. Refrigerate after cutting into strips. Refrigerate for up to 5 days.

Nutrition: Calories: 110; Fat: 3 g; Net Carbs: 0 g; Protein: 23 g

137. Dog Ice Cream

Preparation Time: 10 Minutes
Cooking Time: 30 Minutes
Serving: Chihuahua
Ingredients:
- 2 6-ounce containers plain yogurt
- 1 tbsp Honey
- ½ cup carob chips

Directions:
1. All ingredients should be well mixed in a medium basin.
2. Spoon into silicone cupcake liners or an ice cube tray.
3. Wait for two hours till it's firm before freezing.

Nutrition: Calories: 46; Fat: 3.4 g; Net Carbs: 0 g; Protein: 3.8 g

138. Peanut Butter & Carob Swirl

Preparation Time: 10 Minutes
Cooking Time: 30 Minutes
Serving: Poodle
Ingredients:
- 32-ounces plain yogurt
- 1 cup natural peanut butter
- ½ cup carob chips

Directions:
1. In a 24-cup mini muffin pan, distribute yogurt equally among the cups.
2. Combine the carob chips and peanut butter in a microwave-safe bowl.
3. Melt the carob and peanut butter chips in the microwave for 30 seconds, if necessary.
4. Top each muffin cup with a dollop of the peanut butter mixture.
5. Gently whisk or swirl the yogurt and peanut butter together using a toothpick in a "figure 8" pattern.
6. Wait for two hours till it's firm before freezing.

Nutrition: Calories: 310; Fat: 25 g; Net Carbs: 6.7 g; Protein: 13.8 g

139. Bacon Cookies

Preparation Time: 10 Minutes
Cooking Time: 30 Minutes
Serving: Dachshund
Ingredients:
- 1-pound uncured bacon
- 1–2 tbsp chicken or beef broth or bouillon
- 2½ cups whole wheat flour or oats

Directions:
1. Mix everything into a dough.
2. Roll and cut into pieces or cookies.
3. Bake for 30 minutes.

Nutrition: Calories: 190; Fat: 8.9 g; Net Carbs: 18.2 g; Protein: 10.8 g

140. Carob Dog Biscuits

Preparation Time: 10 Minutes
Cooking Time: 30 Minutes
Serving: Dachshund
Ingredients:
- 2 cups Coconut Flour
- 1 tbsp Coconut Oil
- 1 cup Peanut Butter, smooth
- ½ cup Carob Chips melted
- 1 cup Coconut milk
- 1 tbsp Maple syrup
- 1 tsp baking powder
- ½ tsp baking soda

Directions:
1. Preheat the oven to 350°F.
2. In a mixing bowl, combine the baking soda, flour, and baking powder.
3. In a separate bowl, combine the peanut butter, maple syrup, and coconut milk.
4. Combine both mixtures and drop by spoonfuls onto a baking sheet.
5. Bake for 25 minutes and set aside to cool.
6. Melt the carob chips and coconut oil in a saucepan.
7. Set aside the carob chips mixture to cool. Dip the cookies into the mixture.
8. After the biscuits have cooled, serve them.

Nutrition: Calories: 164; Fat: 11 g; Net Carbs: 12 g; Protein: 4 g

141. Basic Dog Biscuits

Preparation Time: 10 Minutes
Cooking Time: 30 Minutes
Serving: Dachshund
Ingredients:

- 1 Egg
- 2 cups Flour, whole wheat which is great for dogs that can consume oats or white flour
- ½ cup, hot water
- ½ tsp Salt
- 1 tsp Chicken bouillon powder

Directions:

1. Preheat oven to 350°F.
2. Dissolve the bouillon in hot water and add the remaining ingredients.
3. Knead the dough for approximately 3 minutes until a ball has formed. Roll the dough to a thickness of ½ inch. Cut the dough with a bone-shaped cookie cutter.
4. Grease a cookie sheet lightly and place cookies on it.
5. Let bake for a minimum of 30 minutes.

Nutrition: Calories: 176; Fat: 3 g; Net Carbs: 3 g; Protein: 17 g

142. Popsicles with Blueberries

Preparation Time: 10 Minutes
Cooking Time: 30 Minutes
Serving: Beagle
Ingredients:

- 1 pound (450g) blueberries
- 1 cup plain low-fat yogurt

Directions:

1. In a blender, puree the blueberries and yogurt.
2. Fill an ice cube tray halfway with the mixture.
3. Freeze for at least 24 hours. Transfer frozen cubes to a zip-top plastic bag and keep them in the freezer for up to 2 months.

Nutrition: Calories: 221; Fat: 7.4 g; Net Carbs: 13.1 g; Protein: 25.3 g

143. Banana Ice Cubes

Preparation Time: 10 Minutes
Cooking Time: 30 Minutes
Serving: Beagle
Ingredients:

- 1 banana, very ripe
- 1 cup water

Directions:

1. Slice the banana into pieces and put them into an ice cube tray.
2. Fill with water. The overly ripe, mushy bananas will permeate the entire ice cube with their flavor.
3. Freeze for at least 24 hours. Transfer frozen cubes to a zip-top plastic bag and keep them in the freezer for up to 2 months.

Nutrition: Calories: 225; Fat: 10 g; Net Carbs: 14.2 g; Protein: 16 g

144. Raw Nuggets

Preparation Time: 10 minutes
Freezing time: 24 hours
Serving: Labrador Retriever
Ingredients:

- 1 pound (450 g) lean ground turkey, lamb, or beef, uncooked
- ¼ cup fresh parsley, chopped
- ¼ cup alfalfa sprouts, chopped
- ¼ cup sesame seeds

Directions:

1. Combine the meat, parsley, and sprouts in a mixing dish.
2. Make small balls with a size of 1" (2.5cm) out of the mixture. Sprinkle sesame seeds on top. Continue until all of the ingredients have been utilized.
3. Place on a plate or baking tray and freeze for a few hours. Once the balls have been frozen, place them in airtight containers. They can be kept in the freezer for up to 6 months.

Nutrition: Calories: 335; Fat: 17 g; Net Carbs: 0 g; Protein: 45 g

145. Homemade blackberry biscuits

Preparation Time: 10 Minutes
Cooking Time: 30 Minutes
Serving: Shetland Sheepdog
Ingredients:
- 1 egg
- 4 cups almond meal
- ¼ cup flax meal
- ½ cup Blackberries
- ¼ cup Olive oil
- 1 cup water

Directions:
1. Set the oven to 350°F.
2. The baking sheet should be lined with parchment paper.
3. The ingredients should be combined to create a dough.
4. Cut biscuit shapes from rolled-out dough.
5. Bake for 30 minutes.
6. Cool, then serve.

Nutrition: Calories: 140; Fat: 7 g; Fiber: 6 g; Carbs: 22 g; Protein: 7 g

146. Homemade Doggie Pops

Preparation Time: 10 Minutes
Cooking Time: 30 Minutes
Serving: Chihuahua
Ingredients:
- 1 cup blueberries, whole
- ½ cup strawberries, chopped
- 1 cup plain Yogurt.

Directions:
1. Ingredients are combined in a bowl.
2. The mixture should be poured into prepared molds.
3. Freeze for 4–5 hours.
4. Take away and serve.

Nutrition: Calories: 70.8; Fat: 1.2 g; Net Carbs: 1 g; Protein: 14g

147. Frozen Peanut Butter Banana Treats

Preparation Time: 10 Minutes
Cooking Time: 30 Minutes
Serving: Poodle
Ingredients:
- 4 cups plain yogurt
- 2 tbsp peanut butter
- 3 bananas, peeled and mashed

Directions:
5. Puree all of the ingredients together.
6. Fill plastic cups or ice cube trays with the mixture.
7. Freeze until solid.
8. It keeps in the freezer for 2 weeks and is a tasty treat.

Nutrition: Calories: 280; Fat: 10 g; Carbs: 26 g; Protein: 3 g

148. Bacon Peanut Butter Biscuits

Preparation Time: 10 Minutes
Cooking Time: 30 Minutes
Serving: Poodle
Ingredients:

- 1 cup Peanut butter, creamy and unsalted
- ¾ cup milk
- 1 Egg
- 2 cups whole wheat flour
- ⅓ cup Oats, rolled
- 3 strips Bacon, cooked and chopped

Directions:

1. Preheat the oven to 325°F. Lightly grease a cookie sheet.
2. In a mixing bowl, combine the peanut butter, oats, milk, egg, and bacon. Mix in the flour and baking powder until the mixture forms a thick dough. Knead the dough lightly on the counter to thoroughly combine the ingredients. (If needed)
3. On a lightly floured surface, roll out 14 of the dough and cut with a bone-shaped cookie cutter.
4. Arrange evenly on a cookie sheet. Cook for 18–20 minutes at 350°F. Remove a cookie sheet from the oven and flip the cookies with a spatula. Bake for 10 minutes more, or until lightly browned.
5. Allow cooling before serving as a treat to your dog. Refrigerate for a week or store at room temperature.

Nutrition: Calories: 251.4; Fat: 9.2 g; Net Carbs: 34.1 g; Protein: 11.2 g

149. Basic Baked Chicken Treats

Preparation Time: 10 Minutes
Cooking Time: 30 Minutes
Serving: Beagle
Ingredients:

- 1 10-ounce can chicken with liquid
- 2 eggs
- 1 cup tapioca flour
- ½ cup white flour
- 1 tbsp coconut oil

Directions:

1. Preheat the oven to 350°F.
2. Blend chicken and eggs.
3. Pour in a bowl and stir in flour and oil.
4. Spread into the desired mold.
5. Bake for 12 minutes.
6. Once cooled, remove the treats from the mold.
7. Refrigerate or freeze and feed as a treat.

Nutrition: Calories: 200; Fat: 13 g; Protein: 5g; Carbs: 18g

150. Raw Vegetable Cupcakes

Preparation Time: 10 Minutes
Cooking Time: 30 Minutes
Serving: Bulldog
Ingredients:

- 1 celery head, trimmed
- 1 pack carrots
- 1/3 cup parsley
- 1 Romaine lettuce or mustard greens

Directions:

1. Clean and cut the vegetables.
2. Cut into squares and purée in a food processor or blender, 1 cup at a time, adding water as needed.
3. Once all of the vegetables have been puréed, place them in an ice cube or cupcake tray to freeze. Transfer to a zip-top plastic bag or an airtight container and freeze for up to 6 months.
4. Serve as a frozen treat or allow to thaw to room temperature before serving.

Nutrition: Calories: 267; Fat: 12 g; Carbs: 43 g; Protein: 15 g

151. Pumpkin & Peanut Butter Rounds

Preparation Time: 15–20 minutes
Cooking Time: 40 minutes
Cooling time: 40–45 minutes
Serving: Beagle
Ingredients:

- 2 cups whole wheat flour
- ½ cups buckwheat flour
- 2 medium eggs
- ½ cup pumpkin puree (fresh or canned—if can make sure it's not seasoned or spiced)
- 2 tbsp dog-friendly peanut butter
- 1 tsp honey
- ½ tsp kosher salt
- ¼–½ tsp ground cinnamon

Directions:

1. Preheat the oven to 350°F.
2. In a small mixing bowl, combine the eggs, salt, cinnamon, and honey; set aside.
3. Sift both flours into a larger mixing bowl.
4. Combine the pumpkin puree, peanut butter, and whisked egg mixture.
5. To make the dough more workable, you may need to add a little water.
6. The dough should not be overly moist or wet; it should be dry and stiff.
7. Roll the dough into a 12-inch strip or roll, then cut it into 12-inch-thick pieces. *If you have a larger dog, roll it and cut it into 1-inch pieces, but the yield will be less* Place on a greased baking sheet and bake for 40 minutes, or until hard.

Nutrition: Calories: 211; Fat: 10 g; Protein: 3g; Carbs: 7 g

152. Raw Crunchy Treats

Preparation Time: 10 Minutes
Cooking Time: 30 Minutes
Serving: Beagle
Ingredients:

- 1 pound (450g) lean ground turkey, lamb, or beef, uncooked
- ¼ cup molasses
- 1 egg
- ½ cup chopped pumpkin seeds

Directions:

1. Combine the meat, egg, and molasses in a large mixing basin.
2. Pour down the chopped raw pumpkin seeds on a flat surface.
3. Form the meat mixture into 1" (2.5cm) balls by pinching off little pieces with your hands. Coat the balls with chopped pumpkin seeds to give them a crunchy texture.
4. Place on a plate or baking tray and freeze for a few hours. Once the balls have been frozen, place them in airtight containers. They can be kept in the freezer for up to 6 months.

Nutrition: Calories: 208.3; Fat: 8.5 g; Net Carbs: 14.5 g; Protein: 18.6 g

153. Crouton Treats

Preparation Time: 10 minutes
Cooking Time: 40 minutes
Serving: Golden Retriever
Ingredients:
- 6 large bread slices
- ½ cup Parmesan cheese, grated
- ½ cup bacon fat or olive oil

Directions:
1. Preheat the oven to 250°F (120°C).
2. Cut the bread into 1-inch-square (2.5-cm) squares.
3. In a large mixing bowl, combine the bread squares and Parmesan cheese. While mixing, drizzle olive oil or bacon fat over the bread cubes to coat them all.
4. Make the croutons according to the package directions and place them on a baking sheet. Bake for 40 minutes, flipping halfway to ensure even browning.
5. Remove the croutons from the oven and set them aside to cool before serving or storing them in the refrigerator.

Nutrition: Calories: 459; Fat: 7 g; Fiber: 4 g; Carbs: 32 g; Protein: 32 g

154. Carrot Cake Crunch Biscuits

Preparation Time: 10 Minutes
Cooking Time: 20 Minutes
Serving: Beagle
Ingredients:
- 2 cups oat flour
- 2 cups brown rice flour
- 1 cup unsweetened additive-free applesauce
- 2 large eggs
- 1 cup peeled & shredded carrots
- ½ cups unsweetened coconut flakes or unsweetened shredded coconut
- ¼ cup dog-friendly nut butter (sometimes I add half almond butter & half peanut butter)
- 1 tsp raw unfiltered honey

Directions:
1. Preheat the oven to 350°F.
2. In a large mixing bowl, combine the applesauce, nut butter, and eggs until smooth.
3. Blend in the flour, carrot shredded, and coconut until the dough stiffens but does not crumble.
4. Knead 3 or 4 times on a lightly floured surface.
5. Roll the biscuit out with a rolling pin until it's 12 inches thick.
6. Shape the treats with cookie or biscuit cutters and place them in a baking pan.
7. Bake for 10 to 20 minutes or until golden brown.
8. Allow about 40 minutes for cooling before serving or storing.
9. Keep it in an airtight container.

Nutrition: Calories: 217; Fat: 7 g; Protein: 8 g; Carbs: 5 g

155. Gluten-free dog treat

Preparation Time: 10 Minutes
Cooking Time: 30 Minutes
Serving: Shetland Sheepdog
Ingredients:
- 1 can pureed pumpkin
- 2 eggs
- 3 cups gluten-free, brown rice, or whole wheat flour
- 3 tbsp peanut butter, xylitol-free
- ½ tsp cinnamon (optional)

Directions:
1. Set the oven's temperature to 350°F.
2. Combine the flour, oats, and cinnamon in a small bowl.
3. Whisk the eggs, pumpkin, and peanut butter together in a separate, big bowl. Mix wet and dry components.
4. Roll the dough to a thickness of ½ inch on a floured surface. Using a cookie cutter, cut out.
5. The dough will be quite sticky; to help, sprinkle some flour on your hands and a rolling pin. Bake for 30 to 35 minutes or until golden brown. Place items on cooling racks and allow them to completely cool. As they cool, they'll become harder.

Nutrition: Calories: 118.2; Fat: 6.7 g; Net Carbs: 13 g; Protein: 2.9 g

156. Banana Frozen Yogurt Treats

Preparation Time: 10 Minutes
Cooking Time: 30 Minutes
Serving: Golden Retriever
Ingredients:
- 4 cups unsweetened yogurt
- 2 tbsp peanut butter, xylitol-free
- 3 ripe bananas, peeled and mashed

Directions:
1. Blend all ingredients into a puree.
2. Transfer to 4-ounce plastic cups (ice trays or toddler popsicle trays work well).
3. Frozen till solid
4. It can last up to 2 weeks in the freezer.

Nutrition: Calories: 380; Fat: 10 g; Net Carbs: 55 g; Protein: 19 g

Chapter 7: Shopping List

- Salmon
- Liver
- Eggs & Dairy
- Squash
- Pumpkin
- Fish
- Milk
- Beef
- Lamb
- Chicken
- Turkey
- Peanut butter
- Spinach
- Kales
- Potatoes
- Sweet potatoes
- Cheese
- Pumpkin
- Blueberries
- Watermelon
- Apple
- Chickpea
- Eggs
- Mango
- Oatmeal
- Carrots
- Chia seeds
- Almond
- Bananas
- Bacon
- Beans
- Bananas
- Apples
- Berries
- Melon
- Papaya
- Meat
- Blueberries
- Apples
- Cranberries
- Fish Oils
- Canola Oil
- Chicken Fat
- Olive Oil
- Liver
- Chia Seeds
- Blueberries
- Pumpkin
- Kale
- Quinoa
- Grains
- Parsley
- Beets
- Turmeric
- Cranberry
- Sage
- Kiwi
- Rice
- Pasta
- Green beans

Conclusion

Thank you for making it to the end of this homemade healthy dog food cookbook. Making homemade dog food takes time and money, but I believe it is completely worth it in the end.

Don't be discouraged if your dog doesn't like the first dish you try. It will take some time to figure out what he or she likes and dislikes. My recommendation is to try a wide variety of foods. It will be a wonderful experience for both you and your dog if you follow the advice and recipes in this book.

Remember that if you're careful with your ingredients, you can simply make an extra serving of whatever you're having for dinner. I'm not sure I'd recommend giving them a seat at the table because dogs, at least mine, don't have that kind of manners.

You can naturally extend your dog's life by feeding him the right food and cooking for him. Discovering homemade dessert recipes is an excellent way to keep your pet healthy and happy. Stay away from commercial snacks as soon as possible and gradually introduce new ones; your pet will adore them. They are, after all, made of real food—meat, vegetables, and grains!

I hope you and your beloved four-legged friend and family member share many special homemade meals for many years to come. This collection of homemade dog recipes can help you get started in providing your dog with some healthy homemade meals; I am sure you will receive many tail-wags and licks of gratitude for serving him these homemade meals.

Good luck.

Recipes Index

A

Almond and Banana Treats   30
Apple Dog Cakes   29

B

Bacon Bites   69
Bacon Cookies   81
Bacon Peanut Butter Biscuits   84
Banana Frozen Yogurt Treats   87
Banana Ice Cubes   82
Basic Baked Chicken Treats   84
Basic Dog Biscuits   82
Beef & Rice   47
Beef and Sweet Potato Stew   32
Beef Chuck and Barley Stew   38
Beef Stew   51
Beef Stock   35
Beef with Apples   42
Beef with Pumpkin   39
Beef, Beans, and Bananas   53
Berry Oatmeal & Pumpkin   23
Bites of Anchovy   66
Blueberry Fruit Rollups   80
Blueberry Muffin   26
Broccoli Beef with Barley   33
Buffalo Meatballs   52

C

Caribbean Canine Coolers   77
Carob Dog Biscuits   81
Carrot Cake Crunch Biscuits   86
Carrot Cake Muffins   27
Carrot Cookies   74
Casserole Slices   72
Cheerios and Peanut Butter Balls   71

Cheese Training Treats   78
Cheesy Beef Meal   56
Cheesy Biscuits   80
Cheesy Eggs and Rice   65
Chia Seed Oatmeal   25
Chicken & Oats   62
Chicken & Sweet Potato   60
Chicken and kales   53
Chicken and Rice   40
Chicken Cake for Dogs   39
Chicken Casserole   46
Chicken Gravy   63
Chicken Jerky   59
Chicken Risotto   75
Chicken Soup   32
Chicken Stew Meal   36
Chicken, Apple, Leafy Medley   73
Chicken, Broccoli, and Rice   38
Chicken, Peas, And Eggs   49
Chickpea Stew   59
Cottage Cheese Breakfast   26
Cranberry Beef   55
Cream Cheese Icing   78
Crouton Treats   86
Crunchy Snacks   72

D

Dehydrated Chicken Liver   59
Deli Turkey Rollups   75
Delicious Chicken Meal   60
Deviled eggs   24
Dog Ice Cream   81
Doggie Meatballs   40
Doggie Meaty   57
Doggie Salmon Balls   41
Dried Beet Chips   68

E

Easter Carrot Cookies 70
Eggshell Dog Meal 63

F

Favorite gourmet meal 49
Fish and Peanut Cookies 68
Fish Pate 54
Fishermen's Eggs 29
Food Pucks 45
Frozen Fruit Popsicles 77
Frozen Peanut Butter Banana Treats 83
Fruit Parfait 69

G

Gluten-free dog treat 87
Gravy with Giblets 51
Green Eggs & Beef 65
Ground Beef and Macaroni 56

H

Healthy Homemade Strips for Dogs 69
Hearty Potato 67
Homemade blackberry biscuits 83
Homemade Dog French omelet 25
Homemade Doggie Pops 83
Homemade Doggie Steak and Liver 38
Homemade Turkey Omelet 29
Hot Chili 71

I

Italian Spinach Balls 66

K

Kale Chips 74
Kale Nachos 75
Kiwi and Canine Kale 70

L

Lamb Hash 52

Lentils 43

M

Mashed Butternut Squash 58
Mashed Potato Icing 79
Max and Penny's Spinach 34
Meat cakes 48
Meat Dog Cake 27
Millet Meal 58
Mini Liver Quiche 24
Mini Pumpkin Muffins 28
Mixed Meat Meal 45

O

Orange Chicken 54

P

Peanut Butter & Carob Swirl 81
Peanut Butter and Banana Dog Ice Cream 80
Peanut Butter Mix 23
Popsicles with Blueberries 82
Potato Chicken Side Dish 73
Pumpkin & Peanut Butter Rounds 85
Pumpkin Balls 37
Pumpkin Cookies 68
Pumpkin Ice Cream 77
Pumpkin Peanut Butter Homemade Dog Treats 79
Pumpkin Rice 34
Pumpkin Treats 80

Q

Quinoa and Kale 44

R

Raw Crunchy Treats 85
Raw Nuggets 82
Raw Vegetable Cupcakes 84
Rice and Green beans 40
Rice and Minced Chicken Meal 44
Rice and Salmon 43

S

Sage Chicken & Sweet Potato 73
Salmon and Spinach Hash 42
Salmon Medley 73
Scrambled Eggs 28
Scrambled Spinach and Salmon 48
Shepherd's Pie 42
Shrimp and Tuna 54
Simple Chicken & Pasta 41
Simple Crispy Cheese 74
Sorbet de Mango 79
Spaghetti Squash with Veggies 61
Spinach Omelet 25
Steak and Broccoli 40
Stir Fry Beef Meal 61
Strips of Dried Beef 62
Sweet Potato & Peanut Butter 23
Sweet Potato Potstickers 71
Sweet Potatoes Meal 62

T

Tahini Fish 35
Thanksgiving meal recipe 50
The Scooby Stew 47
Tofu and Tapioca 37
Triple Three (Chicken, beef, salmon) 37
Tuna Balls 60
Turkey Gravy 55
Turkey Jerky 36
Turmeric Beef 60

V

Vegetable & Turkey Delight 50
Vegetable Bowl 33
Vegetable Fish Patties 65
Vegetable side dish 67

W

Wallace Braveheart's Chicken Meatloaf 57
Watermelon Slush 77
White Meat Mix 46
Woof Loaf 49

References

Besides our knowledge and experiences, I used the following awesome sources to create this book:

AKC Staff. (2019, May 29). Foods Your Dog Should Never Eat. Retrieved from https://www.akc.org/expert-advice/nutrition/human-foods-dogs-can-and-cant-eat/

ASPCA. (2015, September 29). Animal Poison Control Alert: The Dangers of Moldy Food. Retrieved from https://www.aspca.org/news/animal-poison-control-alert-dangers-moldy-food

ASPCA. (2019). Food Guarding. Retrieved from https://www.aspca.org/pet-care/dog-care/common-dog-behavior-issues/food-guarding

Battersea Dogs and Cats Home. (2019, July 23). Toxic food for dogs. Retrieved from https://www.battersea.org.uk/pet-advice/dog-care-advice/toxic-food-dogs

Becotte, J. (2018, August 21). Homemade Diabetic Dog Food Recipe - Ruby Stewbie. Retrieved from https://myuntangledlife.com/homemade-dog-food-for-diabetic-dogs/

Bender, A. (2019, January 27). Learn How to Train Your Dog to Stop Begging. Retrieved from https://www.thesprucepets.com/train-a-dog-to-stop-begging-1117892

American Kennel Club: AKC.org

American Society for the Prevention of Cruelty to Animals: ASPCA.org

Association of American Feed Control Officials: TalksPetFood.AAFCO.org

Center for Science in the Public Interest: CSPINET.org

The Dog Food Advisor: DogFoodAdvisor.com

Pet MD: PetMD.com

U.S. Food and Drug Administration: FDA.gov

Brady, C. How Much Should I Feed my dog? Retrieved from https://dogsfirst.ie/raw-faq/how-much-should-i-feed-my-dog/

Brita. (2018, April 24). Dog Dinner Recipe: Fish Cakes. Retrieved from https://foodwithfeeling.com/dog-dinner-recipe-fish-cakes/

Central Garden & Pet. (2018). Dog Training 101 - 4 Phases to Building an Unbreakable Bond with Your Dog. Retrieved from https://www.avodermnatural.com/blog/dog-training-101-best-bond

Daisy the French Bulldog. (2015, June 2). Tasty Tuesday: Pumpkin-Blueberry-Bacon Pupsicles. Retrieved from http://daisythefrenchbulldog.blogspot.com/2015/06/tayuday-pumpkin-blueberry-bacon.html

Damn Delicious. (2018, June 7). DIY Homemade Dog Food. Retrieved from https://damndelicious.net/2015/04/27/diy-homemade-dog-food/

Dog Food Insider. (2016, September 21). 6 Tips For Introducing Your Dog To A New Dog Food. Retrieved from https://www.dogfoodinsider.com/6-tips-introducing-dog-new-dog-food/

Dogster HQ. (2019, May 13). Dog Feeding Schedule: How Many Times a Day Should I Feed My Dog? Retrieved from https://www.dogster.com/dog-food/dog-feeding-schedule

Dyck, A. (2015, December 8). The Best Kind of Protein for Dogs. Retrieved from https://blog.homesalive.ca/the-best-kind-of-protein-for-dogs

Elliott, P. (2019, April 25). Which Fruits Are Safe for Dogs to Eat? Discover the Benefits & Pitfalls. Retrieved from https://petcube.com/blog/dog-fruits/

Emily's Homestead. (2016, August 18). Homemade Dog Food. Retrieved from https://emilyslittlehomestead.com/2014/01/17/homemade-dog-food/

Finlay, K. (2017, March 29). How to Get Your Dog to Eat More Slowly. Retrieved from https://www.akc.org/expert-advice/health/4-ways-to-slow-your-dogs-eating/

Fleming, A.-M. (2018, September 11). Our Favorite Homemade Dog Food Recipes for Senior Dogs. Retrieved from https://dogquality.com/blogs/senior-dog-blog/our-favorite-homemade-dog-food-recipes-for-senior-dogs

Flowers, A. (2018, June 14). Dog Nutrition: Essential Nutrients for Health and Feeding Basics. Retrieved from https://pets.webmd.com/dogs/dog-nutrition#1

Fitbark. (2018, January 8). How to Pick the Best Dog Food. Retrieved from https://www.fitbark.com/blog/how-to-pick-the-best-dog-food/

Golani, T. (2019, July 22). 33 Best Homemade Dog Food Recipes that are Vet Approved. Retrieved from https://www.favorablethings.com/33-best-homemade-dog-food-recipes-that-are-vet-approved/

Pebworth, K. (2022, April 22). **DIY homemade dog food dangers**. Top Dog Tips.

https://topdogtips.com/diy-homemade-dog-food-dangers/

Prey Model Raw (PMR) diets for dogs & cats. *(2022). **Raw Fed and Nerdy.***

https://rawfedandnerdy.com/pmr-diets-for-dogs-and-cats

Prey Model Raw diet: Is it healthy for dogs? *(2022). **Raw Bistro.***

https://rawbistro.com/blogs/raw-bistro/prey-model-raw-diet#:~:text=What%20Is%20Prey%20Model%20Raw,their%20wild%20canine%20counterparts%20eat

Randall, S. (2022, April 22). ***How to store homemade dog food.*** Top Dog Tips. https://topdogtips.com/how-to-store-homemade-dog-food/

Printed in Great Britain
by Amazon

29733371R00053